*The
Universe
Makers*

The Universe Makers;

SCIENCE FICTION TODAY

by *DONALD A. WOLLHEIM*

HARPER & ROW, PUBLISHERS

NEW YORK, EVANSTON, AND LONDON

1817

FOR ELSIE
who shares my personal universe

Contents

vi] *Contents*

The Day It Began to Come True

EVER SINCE the day that I first heard that an atomic bomb had been exploded over Japan I have had the disturbing conviction that we are all living in a science-fiction story. Atomic power and atomic bombs were old stuff to me at the time, for as an ardent science-fiction fan I had known all about them and their potential for at least a decade. But when the bomb was actually invented and used before the founding of the world state (which was the way it was supposed to have been) I knew we were in for it.

I had at that time already acquired a reputation as a science-fiction authority. I had edited and published the first anthology ever published to use the title "science fiction"—the *Pocket Book of Science Fiction* done in 1943. This was the occasion for a phone call on A-Bomb day from a New York radio station asking me to take part in a hastily organized panel discussion of the atomic bomb's significance.

Although this was the first time I had ever been invited to appear on the air, I simply could not bring myself to do so. I was too uneasy about this misuse of atomic power, too unresolved in my feelings that the world had taken one step too many over the edge of the old realism and into the world of the fantastic future. The possibilities loomed menacingly and chaotically before me, and I was not prepared to talk about it. Instead, I recommended that the station call John W. Campbell, Jr., the editor of what was then—and still is—the leading s-f magazine and the kind of man who could talk a blue streak about scientific and pseudo-scientific possibilities.

I felt then, and I have no cause to change my mind, that the world was entering into a science-fiction phase.

Certainly my thoughts that morning were a mixture of elation at the oncoming of a long-heralded science-fiction event and a sort of sickly foreboding over the fact that it had come when it did and in the form it took. That time, you will recall, was at the end of a grim war—the war was still on, though not for much longer—and we had all been promised, through the media of the press and propaganda, the wonders of the victorious world after the foes were vanquished. Much of the propaganda had, as usual, been taken from the stock in trade of science fiction. This helped in the persuasion that time and history had taken a turn into the unreal, into the misty tracks of the "Days to Come" whose heralds had been the lurid-covered magazines we had fought for so crusadingly.

I was of that pioneering group, the fanatical science-fiction fandom of the thirties, who had believed when others scoffed, who had bought these three or four wild-titled and wildly illustrated magazines and kept them alive during the time when they were among the lowest and least of the pulps that crowded the newsstands of those prewar days. We were a small group compared to the legions of science-fiction readers today—and in consequence very much a beleaguered group. Our lives tended to be bent toward each other, our world was a microcosm of our own lives, and we lived in an atmosphere of infinite horizons that could not be communicated to most of the grim and haunted world of the Depression around us.

Science fiction shaped my life and I can truthfully say I am marked by it in every way. Through it and my associations with its readers and writers I have found my profession, my life, my philosophy, my hobby, and, yes, my wife and friends. Fandom—that organized nucleus of readers—has long been split in its approach by two opposing slogans regarding addiction to science fiction. One is "Fandom is Just a God-Damned Hobby." The other is "Fandom is a Way of Life." For me the latter is the fact.

So I recall sitting at my desk after putting down the phone and thinking to myself, what should I do about the bomb? Atomic power—how many times had stories shown what a world of wonders and prosperity would be humanity's if we could tap the infinite power of the atom. Electricity would be virtually free and endless. We could rebuild the world and with such power end poverty, make the world Utopia, and finally climb to the stars. All that was implied by atomic power which, story after story assured us, would be the tap into Nature's own basic resource. Transmutation of the elements would be open to us.

Such had been the promises of atomic power as foreseen in science fiction.

But then there was the use of this same power in the form of a weapon. There would be rays of such devastating potency that disintegration would result. There would be atomic explosions rivaling the sun in terrible intensity.

If I had taken the radio offer, how should I speak? Should I say that it was the most wonderful news of the century—and that all would be utopian from now on? Or should I admit that in the hands of the old politicians and the old unimaginative generals, with the terrifying division of the world into diametrically opposed political philosophies, this power—in its first form as a superbomb dropped upon an enemy city—was something to dread, not to welcome. That henceforth, because the world was not unified and was not idealistically governed, this power was to be a Sword of Damocles hanging over all mankind and darkening the future.

Both sets of visions churned through my mind. I could not resolve it then. I felt, to be blunt about it, sick. I declined to try to resolve my conflict in a few hours.

That was one aspect of science fiction as a world philosophy. I was a believer in futures. To find that what had been a whole railroad yard of possible futures in the thirties had suddenly been narrowed down to a mere two or three sets of rails heading out—and that it was no longer a matter of daydreaming over the pages of fanciful stories but to be the facts of daily living as humanity roared on along one of those nearly parallel tracks carrying me and my own life with it—that was coming to reality too sharply.

A Life for Science Fiction

SCIENCE FICTION does not, of course, deal strictly with the future, but the major part of it does. By constant reading one acquires a group of conceptions of how the future is going to shape up, and also how it should shape up to be pleasant and how it could shape up to be terrifying.

This world we live in is definitely a world that science fiction conjectured in most of its aspects. The facts of our everyday life today were the fantasies of my youth and the years that preceded my youth. Television was prophesied in many science-fiction tales, going back to the dawn of the century, and taken for granted in the writings of the twenties and thirties. Radio had been a wonder thing in the first years of this century and the source of some wonderful tales right up to the thirties.

Airplanes? Many a great story and fascinating novel had been written about the airplanes of the future, about commercial aviation, about private fliers, aerial bombers, sky pirates, war in the air, and planes city-big as well as planes that one could strap to one's shoulders and take flight. The years following 1945 were to see the blossoming of these things.

I recall the World's Fair of 1939 with a display of future roadways showing such marvels as cloverleafs, banked express highways, and so on. When you viewed this science-fictional exhibit, they gave you a button to wear that read "I have seen the future." True, quite true. We are living in that express highway-cloverleaf future, and we all drive it every day. In fact, it's polluting the countryside along with some of the other wonders we all envisioned: supercities, perfected insecticides, jet engines, and giant factories.

We believed in robots. They used to charge around in such daily comic strips as the original Buck Rogers, and it was not uncommon to see robotic things playing the role of Bug Eyed Monster on the covers of such dignified magazines as *Astounding Stories of Super-Science* and similar conservative titles. Robots could be built to have superbrains, and they are among us today in the form of the increasing plague known as computers. The depersonalization of business and industry is going on apace to-day, and that's a science-fiction concept.

We believed above all else in space flight and rockets and the multiplicity of worlds. Today, to be sure, we have the first two. With radio astronomy and constant search we may yet turn up the last. Rockets were also to lead to great events and space flight was to lead to wonderful adventures. The great events are still mainly veiled in military secrecy and the flights through space are militarily controlled and the fliers little more than hard-boiled and endlessly rehearsed test pilot-actors. Not quite the way we saw it, even though science fiction and its followers can truly claim the right to say we started it and we pushed it through.

At least two of the original seven U.S. astronauts admitted to having been science-fiction readers in their formative days. I have learned that one of the three who made that first flight to the moon itself had spent the day before the takeoff reading one of the Ace editions of Edgar Rice Burroughs. (Could it have been *The Moon Maid?*)

Is this the world that science fiction made? I think it is. One bit of research among men of science showed that a high percentage of them had been turned toward their profession through the reading of science fiction in their youth—and some still read it. The ideas we planted, the seeds we sowed (some of them dragon's teeth, yes) are in bloom about us and we are harvesting the results.

The thing that went wrong is that we may be in the wrong story. It looks to me as if we are in that basic science-fiction tale, envisioned in the thirties, where two great world empires contend with each other, leading up to a war which would leave one the victor and thereby establish the one-state world of Earth. Only after that should space flight and meeting with other intelligent beings of other worlds take place. Otherwise, a divided world confronted by a stronger, more advanced single-nation planet might face the same disasters that divided India faced with a united Britain or the tribes of America with a Spanish empire.

It looks as if that is the story we are in. We are in that tale wherein the great inventions were made before the installation of Utopia. That story never had a happy ending.

But hold it . . . let's not get too gloomy all at once. Science fiction makes no hard and fast rules. It may precede history but history never has been known to follow it exactly either. Nor, for that matter, has science.

What should be evident by now is that science fiction is not just a form of literature to be discussed as literature should be discussed—the lives of authors, the lists of their works, the evaluation of their styles. Science fiction is above all a system of ideas. It deals with ideas more than it deals with literary styles. It speculates in futurities and in probabilities. These are what are more to be remembered than the depth of character of its heroes.

Science fiction, then, is judged by the immense variety of its visions and concepts—which are as varied as the potential of humanity is varied and as multifold as the stars in the sky. It is this harvest of wonders, this garden of marvels, this vision of what could be and what could have been that makes science fiction so different and makes its readers marked for life in out-of-the-rut trains of thought.

The phases of being a science-fiction reader can be traced and charted. So many read it for one year, so many for two, so many for life. For instance, reading it exclusively can be as compulsive as a narcotic for a period of an intelligent teen-ager's life. The length of time as I see it—and I have seen and talked with and corresponded with hundreds and hundreds of such readers in my lifetime—is about four or five years of the most intense reading—usually exclusive, all other literature being shoved aside. After that a falling off, rather rapid (often due to college entry or military life or the hard stuff of getting a job for the first time). There is, I suspect, something like an 80 percent turnover in the mass readers of science fiction every five years.

Which isn't bad. It means that a higher and higher percentage of people have been exposed to its mind-tingling and vision-enlarging writings at the most impressionable times of their lives. The effect lingers on in the world around us.

There are the other 20 percent who cling to it. They are the nucleus who keep the magazines alive in bad times, from whose ranks arise the writers of science fiction and the editors too; people like myself.

I was such a young man. I started reading science fiction sporadically from the time I was eleven. I graduated from grammar school to becoming a total reader. It happened during that last day before graduation—that slack day when one still reports to school, but lessons are over and pupils sit around a classroom killing a couple of hours until allowed to go home. On that day I came to school without anything to read. While I was sitting around wondering how to occupy my mind, another student came over—one I scarcely knew, incidentally—and handed me a copy of *Amazing Stories* saying, "I think you'll like this."

That was the issue containing the first installment of A. Merritt's *The Moon Pool*. How right he was! I was hooked on the s-f magazines at that point. Nevertheless, it was a few months before I could raise the funds to keep on buying that magazine—and had depleted the obvious science-fiction books in the local library. In the interim I missed the concluding installments of Merritt's masterpiece and it was not till many years later that I was able to pick up the back numbers I had missed and find out what happened at the Nan Matal on mysterious Ponape Island.

But I do not think I read any other type of fiction from that day on for at least five or six years. (I exclude those books assigned for homework or college necessity, to be sure. I am talking about reading for pleasure.) I had found my niche.

The usual science-fiction devotee tends to be solitary and introverted in his youth. This is not an exact thing, of course, but in a general form it holds true for most of those I have met. They do not run with the pack—they are at home with their noses buried in the pages of speculation. Even if they are of a sociable nature, what they want to talk about is the wealth of wonders they have absorbed through their reading. They find that the average youth is not concerned. A little such talk goes a long way. Whereas the ardent s-f addict will talk about science and Mars and the moon and space flight and time travel all day and all night too, he soon finds that among the friends of his own age there is usually no one he can talk with about this. So he becomes a solitary until he discovers that he can correspond with others like himself. Then he obtains a typewriter and does so for hour after hour.

Such is my own history, for I was definitely that kind of solitary reader, devouring everything the magazines published, every book I could buy or borrow, and eventually writing to other fans and trying to write stories myself. The problems of daily life, getting through school, worrying about college, thinking about making a living, were never as real as the problem of how the moon flight was to be organized, what we would find on Mars, and whether atomic power would be released in our time. That was what counted.

That, to be sure, is what eventually did count. In that sense the stubborn introverted convictions of the s-f fan were ultimately to be proved right. It is that conviction, pursued with the fanaticism of a religious convert, that impressed itself upon so many who were to leave the world of fantastic literature to work in the world of scientific realities—and thereby ultimately produce those things that only some wild pulp writers had spoken of.

So it came about that the friends of my youth were found eventually among dreamers like myself. I corresponded around the country and overseas, and I met and formed clubs with similar types at home.

The history of the world of science-fiction fandom has been written elsewhere and is in any case not relevant to this book. Suffice it to say that I became prominent in that microcosm, that through it I was to determine my life trade—that of a writer and editor, and to find work in those fields. Through it also I was to meet the girl that I married and to establish my place in society.

Like many of my fellow introverts I wanted to write out my own angles of these fantastic conjectures. I had the remarkable fortune to sell the first story I ever wrote, a short piece, to Hugo

Gernsback's *Wonder Stories*. That was in 1933 and from that time on I knew that science fiction was not to be just a reading hobby but also a life interest.

I became a full-time professional editor in 1941, putting out two magazines for a shoestring publisher. My budget was nothing, literally nothing. Stories were solicited from my friends, art work was cajoled from fan artists with professional ambitions. The magazines lasted a year or so, long enough to gain me a "foot in the door" as a pro editor (at no salary), and get me hired on as a pulp magazine editor for A. A. Wyn, who had a chain of such magazines under the "Ace" imprint.

But don't think those two magazines I edited so cheaply were full of unknowns. It was in their pages that such writers as C. M. Kornbluth, Robert Lowndes, and others first made their mark, and our chief artist was Hannes Bok, who has a whole movement devoted to his name today.

It was shortly after joining Wyn (where I edited detectives, westerns, and sports magazines, but not fantasy) that I conceived and sold the first two anthologies directly dealing with science fiction, the aforementioned *Pocket Book of Science Fiction* and the *Viking Portable Novels of Science*. On the basis of those I was later to sell Avon Books the idea of a series of similar anthologies—the *Avon Fantasy Readers*—which led me to joining their staff and finding myself almost immediately their editor (by virtue of the fact that the man who hired me quit two months later). For two years thereafter there was no person in the entire editorial staff save myself. I was it—first reader and editor in chief and official and only blurb and caption writer. I will drop that line of discussion right here too—what happened to me at Avon and after is another book, which discretion indicates I ought to write only after retiring.

3

A Matter of Plausibility

LET US get back to science fiction. Before we go any further I had better define what I mean by it. How do I know when such and such a work is science fiction and when it isn't? When I first thought about writing this present book the *New York Times* list of the ten hard-cover best sellers had three titles that I considered to be science fiction. Of these the authors of two would probably have winced at the label, while the third could not have squirmed out of it.

The books were *The Andromeda Strain* by Michael Crichton, *Slaughterhouse Five* by Kurt Vonnegut, Jr., and *Ada* by Vladimir Nabokov. The last two authors are the ones that would have winced. The first title is unmistakably standard s-f.

What, then, is my definition of science fiction? There have been many attempts to define science fiction . . . you can find them in the introductions to anthologies and they all differ a little from each other. I do not agree with all of them—I think most anthologists are too restrictive, too tight, in their definitions. Back in 1935 I did a short article for a fan magazine in which I set forth my own definitions of the three classifications of adult fantasy:

> Science fiction is that branch of fantasy, which, while not true of present-day knowledge, is rendered plausible by the reader's recognition of the scientific possibilities of it being possible at some future date or at some uncertain period in the past.
>
> Weird fiction is that branch of fantasy dealing with supernatural or occult subjects, which is rendered plausible by the reader's recognition of the fact that there are people somewhere who at present, or in the past, did believe, or do believe in the truth of the ideas therein and is therefore willing to concede the truth of these things for the period in which he is reading the story.

Pure fantasy is that branch of fantasy which, dealing with subjects recognizable as nonexistent and entirely imaginary, is rendered plausible by the reader's desire to accept it during the period of reading.

As you see, these definitions are based upon the reader's voluntary will to believe. Plausibility is the necessary factor in all reading, mainstream as well as fantasy. To make a fantastic premise plausible one must utilize one of these three approaches. Depending upon which one you use, the classification must follow inevitably.

In the case of *The Andromeda Strain*, the premise is that a space probe satellite returns to earth contaminated by a strain of germs originating outside this planet. Although the novel is virtually newspaper stuff, its success is certainly based upon remarkable timing—for it hit the stores coincidentally with the return of the Apollo 11 astronauts to quarantine precisely to isolate and offset any lunar germs they might have picked up on the moon. The story is science-fictional in that it deals with a space probe that did pick up such a germ and what happened when it returned to contaminate a small Nevada village. The author packed it with seemingly authentic details about what are supposed to be present-day procedures in handling space probes—and since many of these procedures are still cloaked by the secrecy that blacks out much of today's scientific enterprise connected with the military, the author's depiction of what he thought those procedures were seemed both very real and very probable.

I note here that this work—which I personally found absolutely engrossing, for Crichton knows how to spin a suspense story—has been torn apart by s-f magazine reviewers for absurdities in plot and premise. I cannot criticize their objections for they make sense, but the novel was still a spellbinder and its best-seller status easily understood.

Vonnegut's *Slaughterhouse Five*, though directed at the mainstream reader, is, like most of Vonnegut's writing, a sharp-edged satire. With a grim sardonic touch, the acid edge of contrast between horror and farce, the novel tells of the bombing of Dresden in World War II through the medium of a modern middle-class American who is afflicted with a distortion of his time sense. He shifts back and forth between present, past, and future, and is also the pawn and puppet of alien intelligences from a planet somewhere else in the galaxy.

The utilization of this extraterrestrial manipulation makes the work science fiction. The public has been sold already on the probable existence of alien intelligences around other stars and also on the possibility of switching back and forth in time. Vonnegut does not neglect his science-fictional argumentation for these premises either. Hence, the work is science fiction.

Lest someone now raise the objection that Vonnegut throws his star people at us cold, I will say that one s-f premise builds and grows upon the body of s-f lore and argument that has gone before. This I will discuss at length later.

As for *Ada,* a work manifestly not intended for the science-fiction audience, and, for that matter, not very readable to the average person since Nabokov is one of the elite literary multi-level observationists, the background of the long novel is laid on what is known in s-f as a parallel world. This is one where the Russians found and colonized North America first, and *Ada's* world is a United States not too terribly different from our own save that what would be of Anglo-Saxon root in our real land is of Russian root in Nabokov's. At one point in the novel a character indulges in a long pseudo-scientific speculation on the possibility of a parallel world wherein the English colonized America and what that world would be like—in short a description of our world.

This puts the book squarely into the realm of s-f, not of pure fantasy. For here Nabokov has built upon a whole stratum of s-f novels arguing the premise that there is a multitude of parallel worlds, all Earths, spaced apart by some alteration of molecular count or dimensional layerage, and in these other Earths history would have worked out according to other alternates of history. These "Worlds of If," to give them a popular generic name, are an increasing favorite in modern s-f writing. They afford grand fun for sociological speculation, not to mention fine arenas for heroic adventures.

One of the earliest such works, incidentally, was a collection of essay-stories, including one by Winston Churchill, entitled appropriately *If*. I would not define this ancestral work as science fiction, however, for Churchill made no effort to justify his alternate history—it was a take it or leave it presentation, in short, "pure fantasy" classification.

Let's play this string out a little more. It should be apparent that it is possible to produce the same novel as any one of the three classifications and requires often only a paragraph or two to do it. What may be unacceptable to one reader on a pure fantasy approach may be made acceptable by inventing a reasonable "scientific" premise or an occult one.

Take J. R. R. Tolkien's magnificent trilogy *The Lord of the Rings*. These adventures all take place in a world, plainly not the one we know, which the author calls Middle Earth. Tolkien makes no effort to place this Middle Earth in relation to our own Earth (Upper Earth?). He writes of it, maps it, gives its history, but he does not say anything that could pin it down in any scientific cosmology.

Middle Earth might be taking place in some forgotten past epoch, but Tolkien does not say so and contradictions of speech, time, and anthropology would immediately set in should he make such a claim. It could be a parallel Earth, but he disdains to play that game. It is too much like our own Earth to be acceptable as a planet somewhere else in the universe. Now, it would not have taken Tolkien more than a few paragraphs to have made it science fiction by choosing to utilize such a pseudo-scientific ploy and perhaps alter a few elements in his background to establish it, but he was not so interested. Middle Earth is a place one takes on faith. You believe in Frodo and his quest because a fine work of imaginative writing makes you quite willing to suspend disbelief just to enjoy it. It is pure fantasy, and that is the only classification we can give to *The Lord of the Rings*.

Or, Tolkien could have put it into the weird fantasy classification by some claim that magic does so exist, and that elves and dwarfs and the like are real beings of the supernatural world, and that Middle Earth is the world of "another plane" wherein they dwell. This would have taken even more rewriting than making it science-fictional and might very well have alienated many readers and spoiled a lot of the enjoyment. *The Hobbit*, which was published as a children's book, is probably read by children in exactly that manner—here is a part of fairyland and fairyland is real to the child's mind that does not require more erudite hocus-pocus to establish acceptance.

Andre Norton's six novels of the *Witch World* are an instance wherein a science-fiction springboard was utilized to present a planet as magical and variegated in its own way as Middle Earth. For in the first novel of the series, Simon Tregarth is on Earth escaping from enemies and finds his escape by means of a "Gate" between worlds, operated by its discoverer. We are told quite definitely that it utilizes scientific principles of an ancient and lost galactic race to transfer by means of some sort of instantaneous space warp a thing or a person from one planet of the galaxy to another. The exact location of the Witch World is not known—but it is definitely somewhere in our own space-time continuum, though so remote an area that the laws of science that work there are not quite the same as the ones that work here.

Now this Gate Between Worlds is not an Andre Norton invention either. It is one of those premises upon which science fiction today rests—ideas worked out in the past and now taken for granted when utilized today.

Science fiction is built upon such premises. Somewhere in the early days of the literature someone invented a premise, argued it out with scientific (or more likely pseudoscientific) logic and convinced the readers. Once the argument is made, the premise is at once accepted on its own word, enters the tool shed of the science-fiction writer, and may be utilized thereafter by any craftsman without further repetition of the operational manual.

As a boy I was fascinated by L. Frank Baum's Oz books. One of the things that has always struck me about those books, which may be part of the underlying reason for their popularity among American children of the twentieth century, is that they come exceedingly close to being science fiction. Baum set out to write a distinctly American version of a fairy tale, and unconsciously he hit upon plausibility premises close to the s-f mark. Oz is sometimes described as being on a parallel world, almost in those words. People from America get there through various means, often natural catastrophes, which could be easily science-fictionized into Gates Between Worlds. Dorothy gets there at one time by means of a tornado, at another through falling into the inside of the Earth via an earthquake, once thrown overboard at sea in a fierce storm and washed ashore near Oz. Similar means have been utilized by s-f writers to present Gates Between Worlds.

Even the magic and witchcraft of Oz smacks of science fiction, for it has to be learned, it follows the books of lore, it can be taught (the Wizard is taught by Glinda), and one needs scientific instruments to practice it.

I am not claiming the Oz books as science fiction, however, because they are still too much fairy tale. What I am demonstrating is that a little ingenuity and borrowing from the established propositions of past s-f writing could make them so.

Take this gimmick of the Gates Between Worlds. I have already said that one explanation for this device is the supposition of a space warp. Space warps themselves are another gimmick too, worked out in detail in someone's past fiction, at least forty years ago. The idea is that space is not continuous but may be wrinkled—"warped" sounds more scientific. Hence the argument runs: two segments of space may be separated by thousands of light years traveling along the visible three-dimensional continuum of space, yet may be touching each other because space or the universe or something is wrinkled and the two sections are touching each other like two pages of a book. The Gate then is merely an extradimensional means of cutting across this touching point and thereby avoiding the problem of having to travel those thousands of light years inch by inch.

That's one argument. There are many more, worked out by inventive writers. Another and equally prominent argument is that the Gate Between Worlds is an automatic matter-transmitter which operates like a radio or television, that is, instead of transmitting the electronic pattern of sound or sight it breaks down matter into its own electronic patterns, broadcasts them to a station elsewhere, and reassembles the pattern there into a total facsmile of the original—life and all. The *transmatter* isn't all that simple and the possibilities of confusion are endless and so are the stories that have been built upon it.

The point that I am stressing is that modern science fiction no longer requires an author to go into all this argument. He has only to say he has a Gate or a transmatter and the reader is able to supply from memory of past stories all the plausibility quotient he needs to accept this as a future probable invention.

Science fiction builds upon science fiction. As a result of this, modern stories are freer to deal with sociological possibilities and the movement of humanity under future conditions and do not have to repeat pseudoscientific propositions endlessly.

4

Verne or Wells?

SCIENCE FICTION breaks into four major classifications and any story may fit one or several of these groupings:

> Imaginary Voyages
> Future Predictions
> Remarkable Inventions
> Social Satire

Under Imaginary Voyages come trips to the moon and planets and stars, trips to the prehistoric past or the center of the earth, voyages to unexplored parts of this world such as *Gulliver's Travels* and *She*, visits to the infinitely small and the infinitely large, trips to the future, and so on.

Future Predictions covers the stories that tell you what could be happening to mankind tomorrow or in the next century or a million years from now, here or wherever in the universe, with or without man, come to think of it. Mainly it tends to involve genuine accounts of what could happen if such and such a trend or potential continues or comes to pass. Utopias are a variety of this (though they may also be found as Imaginary Voyages), as well as wars to come, or plagues, or famines. Trips to the planets obviously are both Future Predictions and Imaginary Voyages, and probably ought to include the next category of Remarkable Inventions.

In this classification would come many stories taking place in the present where we assume something has been discovered. *The Invisible Man* is an example. Again Remarkable Inventions usually are found in the previous two classifications as well.

Social Satire generally partakes of one or all of the previous classifications, but is· a class by itself because of the motivation of the writer. The intent is to hold a mirror to the present, by means of the future or of an imaginary land, and thereby either make fun, a dire prediction, a somber warning, or a healthy look at where we are all going and What Does It All Mean. *Gulliver's Travels* is a good specimen of that, and *1984* also. In Social Satire science fiction becomes a means to an end but is not the end itself, as it may be in the previous classifications.

Social Satire of the past was often rather obvious and crude. The best of modern s-f usually contains a touch of it, but neither crudely nor always obviously either. Where science fiction has meaning beyond its momentary entertainment value may depend exactly on the combination of logical future prediction and compassionate social satire that the writer is able to bring to bear upon it, without being soapboxy about it.

In fact it may be said that much of the talk that goes on between full-time science-fiction writers about their ever-recurrent dream of someday being accepted fully into the mainstream of literature must derive from their awareness of the implicit social criticism of their projections. The best of modern science fiction carries social satire elements which, it must be pointed out at once in fairness to definitions, do not appear to be satirical in the old sense. Any effort to imagine what people will think and do in unrealized situations of unattained conditions can only be described as a form of satire. The reality never quite jibes.

A great deal of what seems to be maturity in modern s-f derives from its combination of these four elements in the same story, plus, to be sure, writing above the level of a penny-a-word hack.

But good writing is not a monopoly of recent authors. The quality of writing depended upon the men who were attracted to this sort of work. It is just that today, in an environment reeking of science fiction on every side and in every headline, the number of good talents being attracted is vastly greater than back in the wood-paneled airless parlors of the nineteenth century.

Verne was a first-rate writer for his day, though his work was intended primarily for juvenile readers. It is impossible to read him today without realizing that he had a talent for detail of background equal to any, that his eye for the nuances of his time was up to the level of any—it is in his dialogue and his characterizations that the juvenile level shows up strongly.

I am not here writing a history of science fiction—this has been done by others—and I recommend such studies as those of I. F. Clarke, W. H. G. Armytage, H. Bruce Franklin, and most of all Sam Moskowitz for detailed exposition of that sort. I am concerned with the flow of ideas that grew as a result of all this. So here I shall start with the two who are always listed in quick surveys as the fathers of the field—Jules Verne and H. G. Wells.

A basic divergence that can be detected through science fiction can be traced to the thinking of these two. Others wrote concurrently with them, but these two are the ones that stood out, these are the ones we remember and whose works remain available to be read as part of the beginning heritage of those who came later to the field. We know that original conceptions credited to both Verne and Wells could be traced in earlier writers—Sam Moskowitz has done a good deal of that—but it is not the misty records of medieval mariners who may or may not have sailed across the Atlantic that we remember, it is the voyage of Columbus that "fixed" the event and from which the New World derives. Similarly, submarine voyages may have been invented and described by earlier writers, but it is *Twenty Thousand Leagues Under the Sea* which we recall as the one that set the scene in the s-f pantheon.

Verne turned out a flock of remarkable premises for science fiction (or at least he produced the successful popularizations for them). In his writings can be traced not merely the submarine but the airship and the airplane, rocket weapons, voyages around the moon, telecommunication, power locomotion, city planning, and so forth. But whatever his projection, his scenes and his characterizations never changed—they were always reflected against the unvarying political scenery of the latter half of the nineteenth century. There is no evidence of social change in his works—his inventions do not change their inventors nor their users. Sometimes one like Captain Nemo or Robur may dedicate himself to righting wrongs, but the motivation even then is usually revenge or personal vindication rather than any soaring desire to move the human condition forward.

Jules Verne was and remained to the end a typical small-minded French bourgeois nationalist. His works reflect no other thinking. He saw other nationalities in the typical caricature traits common to the most vulgar political thinking of his time. He was quite capable of the crudest anti-Germanism (a product of the defeat of 1871) and the kind of cheap anti-Semitism which ultimately culminated in the French national disgrace of the Dreyfus Affair.

Verne's works stayed tightly within the restrictions of Imaginary Voyages and Remarkable Inventions, and strayed into Future Predictions with great reluctance, and into Social Satire never.

On the other hand, H. G. Wells started off in the realm of Future Prediction and Social Satire with his magnificent gem *The Time Machine*, still one of the most perfect little novels in the genre. I read this one in the public library at the age of ten, gaining the perspective of humanity carried on, changing, evolving, and perhaps disappearing as millions of years passed, and its internal differences brought about the emergence of two humanities—neither desirable, neither destined for immortality. This was social satire and unforgettable future prediction. This was Wells's introduction to the world, for it was his first great novel, the one he had written and rewritten since his school days, whose polish and concept reflected vividly the potential of the social struggle upon which the turn of the twentieth century pivoted.

Wells was a Utopian and though his writings were to encompass as many Remarkable Inventions as Verne—indeed to help fill out the armory of modern science fiction—it was his Social Satire that was dearest to his heart and was the lever with which he sought to move the world.

Even such apparent Imaginary Voyages as his *War of the Worlds* and *The Island of Dr. Moreau* are enhanced by his use of these themes—invasion from space and the biological restructuring of beasts into humanoids—not merely for shock and thrill-a-minute purposes as would have been done by Verne and the others of his ilk. They are asparkle with implications of social thinking, with mirrors held up to our mind and the suggestion to think not merely of the horror but of what should be done to change our philosophy of the universe.

One can go through the works of Wells and pick out the original concepts that seem to be "firsts" in the foundations of modern science fiction. Not merely the two listed above, and the time machine as well, but also a myriad others such as can be found by a perusal of his short stories.

My copy of *The Short Stories of H. G. Wells* is one of my personal treasures for it was a presentation to me from my mother on my fifteenth birthday. It has been read and reread innumerable times. From it I have derived many of the elements that have influenced my thinking and my life, and not the least of these was the style of writing. My short stories are not many, but they have been cast in the premise set forth by Wells, that a good story of science fiction should have but one theme that departs from the accepted and credible. Against a background of the known, one unknown factor gains impact and is best set off.

Going over the short stories of H. G. Wells strictly for Remarkable Inventions we encounter first after first in the realm of s-f basics: rivalry of insect "civilization" with humanity, war tanks, man-eating plants, diamond making, collision with another star, superacceleration of life, the shop of marvels, the man with psi talents, worship of science, germ development, travel beyond this dimension, and on and on. And if one adds the novels, we find aerial warfare, the bedlam of the over-crowded future city, size-changing foods, and atomic power.

For Remarkable Inventions, Wells had it all over Verne. For Imaginary Voyages, he was moderately deficient, but in the other two categories he soared. Therein lay the talent that put H. G. Wells into his permanent position in the world of great literature.

Wells started as something of a social alarmist, but he rapidly developed into a Utopian, a Fabian Socialist at first, a World Stater toward the end. Wellsian Socialism is a vague term—it seems to mean a combination of scientific achievement for the betterment of mankind and utilized on a social basis. It was always rather misty, expressed in general ideas, aspirations, but rarely clear enough to enable any reader to tie in with any specific social movement. Wells, to be sure, wrote innumerable political tracts, but the world of the science-fiction reader has never paid attention to them. They were destined to be outdated with great speed and are today antiquities dealing with things that seem to have no relation to today's world. But his science fiction remains the means by which he continues to influence the world. The very method he abandoned for political lecturing turned out ultimately to be his sole lasting memorial, an inextricable part of the science-fiction world that is today.

It is possible to theorize that, as in *The Time Machine*, Verne and Wells produced two diverging evolutions in science-fiction writing and thinking and that this can be detected in the dichotomy between *Analog* magazine and its competitors in the form of *Galaxy*, *If*, and *Magazine of Fantasy & Science Fiction* . . . and, yes, *New Worlds* too.

Consider the two: Verne, the small-minded nationalist without social content and with a fixation only on inventions and gadgets. Wells, the Utopian, concerned with social aspirations and world organization and always utilizing science fiction in context with its influence on the changing of humanity. Does it not seem that Verne would inevitably lead to a magazine like *Analog*, whose editorials, which dominate the magazine and color its contents, reflect a similarly small-minded nationalist thinking, whose stress is on gadgets and inventions, and which consciously rejects Utopianism and the changing of "human nature" to adjust to changing technologies and infinite worlds? *Analog*, which is a magazine I discuss later at greater depth, is prepared to accept alterations in all the scientific laws whether physics, chemistry, biology, or astronomy, but never in what the editor believes to be the laws of economics—which are forever fixed, perfect, immutable, and not to be questioned.

Whereas in the contents of *Analog's* various rival magazines, put out by many editors and many publishers, no such fixation appears. The range and scope of stories in *Galaxy* and the *Magazine of Fantasy & Science Fiction* is wide open, and therein the laws of economics are as subject to change as any other. It is accepted that the better the writing the more likely will be reflected the social and psychological changes in man and mankind caused by projected futures or inventive situations. Here in these magazines and their writers seems to be reflected the other current, the Wellsian current, which says there is no scientific advancement without its impact on humanity.

It is not an accident that the one magazine espouses racism in its ugliest form, puts forth arguments in favor of slavery (Yes, I said slavery!), and insists on the deliberate revision of stories to include statements of the right of financial greed to triumph over idealistic ideas.

It is not an accident that the other magazines reject racism, cannot even conceive of anyone in this day and age seriously supporting slavery, and ask nothing of their writers save their honest opinions.

It might be argued by Verne readers that Jules Verne did write about Utopianism in his novel *The Begum's Fortune,* wherein two opposing scientific cities were set up in an unpopulated area of Oregon territory, one French, peaceful, intellectual, the other German, mechanized, war oriented. But Verne was just exercising his bent for nationalism and also playing around with the science of architecture and city planning. Of social content—nothing different from the political caricatures of the day.

It might also be argued that Wells did not invent Utopianism

. . . the 1890's were a very fertile area for Utopian writings and Bellamy's *Looking Backward* made a bigger splash in its day than ever Wells did. It was Wells who had the firmest grasp of the century to come—that science would alter it more than someone's armchair social theorizing. *Looking Backward* is pitifully antiquated in style and ideas today. Wells is still an influence.

But there are others who influenced the current of science fiction. One of these influences is the writer Ray Cummings.

As I see it, Ray Cummings bridged the gap between the era of H. G. Wells and the dawn of the science-fiction magazines which crystallized the name and the genre and to which everything modern can be traced.

5

Master of the Microcosm

VERNE wrote in the latter half of the nineteenth century. Wells wrote from 1895 to about 1920 (speaking of him as a science-fiction novelist and short-story writer only). Ray Cummings started in 1920 and his most fruitful period ran through to the late 1930's. He wrote for the pulp magazines, mostly for *Argosy All-Story* weekly and its successor, *Argosy* weekly. That fabulous variety pulp had a style all its own. It ran four serials an issue, one starting, one ending, and two in-between installments. It ran from four to six short stories or novelettes as well. In its pages appeared many of the popular writers of the twenties and thirties, including Edgar Rice Burroughs, Otis Adelbert Kline, Murray Leinster, A. Merritt, and Ray Cummings.

Cummings would have to be described as a Vernian. I know of no Utopias from him. I can think of nothing that could be called a serious sociological prediction. His novels were adventure novels, on a rather simplistic level at that. As likely as not his plot would be that of the heroic scientific young man going to the rescue of a maiden in distress. He had a style all his own, often flowery, given to gasps of wonder and incomplete sentences. He had picked up from Wells's *Time Machine* the trick of often not naming his characters as anything but The Very Young Man, The Businessman, and so on.

But Cummings was grounded in the science of the day, which was that of the early decades of this century. His novels and short stories were expressions of adventure arising from his concept of the universe. This concept is worth analyzing, for therein lies the change in s-f from those days to the present.

During the nineteenth century, and especially in its closing days, there flourished the vision of a purely mechanistic universe. The laws of nature were fixed and permanent and merely awaited their discovery. The planets revolved about the sun in fixed orbits which could be measured and predicted without fear of deviation. The sun moved through the universe in a certain direction at a certain speed and that was that. All suns and comets and galaxies moved on their ways, which could be measured and thereby the universe could be understood. Complex and wonderful it was, but essentially it was like a vast clockwork mechanism which could be mapped and mastered.

In chemistry an observed reaction could be put down on paper and would never thereafter be seen to differ. In physics mathematics proved how one force acted upon another, and that too would always be the case. In biology and geology, evolution had been traced and its course plotted to the present day and simple following of the line could tell us what to expect of future eons.

While many people had expressed doubts about the exactness of all this, by and large mechanistic thinking dominated science. It supplied answers that one could count on in that period of scientific invention—any information to the contrary merely served to obscure thinking. One did not doubt; the glory of the universe was the glory of the watchmaker magnified to infinity, wonderful to think about, and an oyster to be opened by any writer with imagination to open it.

Out of this mechanistic universe came almost all the science fiction of those days, and even after the thirties much of what came along was mechanistic in its application to science.

The mechanistic universe was dealt its death blow by the discoveries of Einstein and by the formula E equals MC squared just as much as our modern political world has been shaken apart by this same formula. Once one realizes that energy and matter are interchangeable, that the transfer of one form to the other is constantly going on, an element of chaos enters the scene. Today's cogwheel could be tomorrow's electrical storm. You can't build a wonder watch on that principle! The formula and the subsequent changing worlds of astronomy, physics, chemistry, biology, and technology have made an awful lot of the old pre-1940 science fiction obsolete. Nevertheless, concepts build upon concepts, and what we have today may be modernized efforts to restructure much of what had been wonders before.

Ray Cummings pioneered in ideas derived from the mechanistic universe that Wells and Verne had neglected. The latter because he probably never thought of it. The former because he was already in 1910 alerted to the coming shift in science, wise to the errors of Victorian science, and not interested in being a writing hack for the popular fiction magazines.

From Ray Cummings we got the fourth dimensional world—that this world could be but one of many divided in space by a fourth dimension incomprehensible to us but verifiable by mathematics. Cummings probed the intriguing possibilities of an age of aviation—his Flyer of Eternal Midnight could be achieved: it was an airliner which flew about the world at the same rate as the world's rotation, arriving at all its ports of call always at midnight. He played around with the concept of robots, the machine men of the future, and they often figured in his tales. Karel Capek had invented the word "robot" for his created humanoids of *R.U.R.*, but they were made of synthetic flesh and blood. Today we use the term "android" for such as these. Robot now means mechanical man, not meat man. Cummings played around with suggestions of space travel to come. I don't think he invented space pirates but he had novels about them.

He certainly played around with past, present, and future, binding them together in a series of novels such as *The Shadow Girl* and *The Man Who Mastered Time.* Wells had invented the time machine, but Cummings put it to full use. In his short stories he brought forth concepts of gravity and size relativity ahead of his time. But what he did best was a type of story which cannot be duplicated today simply because it was based totally on the old mechanistic concepts of space. He traveled to the infinitesimal and to the infinite (and found them both finite).

In his day science knew that matter was composed of electrons and protons, and in the popularizations of the day these were more often compared with miniature solar systems. Electrons of planetary size (comparative) revolved in fixed orbits about protons of solar size. That was it. In the minds of many the further explanation was simple: matter consisted of an infinite number of infinitesimally small solar systems, these systems composed of particles with movements similar to those of the worlds of astronomy.

So it was possible for Ray Cummings to write a novel called *The Girl in the Golden Atom* (Harper & Brothers, 1923) in which his hero, The Very Young Man, goes down in size by means of a pill invented by The Chemist until he is small enough to set foot upon an atomic electron world which then becomes in relation to him just another planet like Earth.

The size-changing pills are one of Cummings' specialties. He used them in many stories thereafter. They are composed of the same material that Alice found in the Drink-Me bottles of Wonderland, albeit Cummings advances pseudoscientific explanations having to do with chemical contraction of tissue and so on.

By means of this gimmick Cummings dares to explore the microcosmic universe. For if these electrons are truly particles of matter revolving about energy-charged sun particles, why, then, they are truly planets and must harbor life and all that accompanies planetary existence.

Ray Cummings' descriptions of his heroes' journeys into smallness are masterpieces of wonder travel. The world grows vast, the viewpoint becomes that of the microscope, then further and gradually, as our hero slips and stumbles over vast rolling molecules like so many marbles in a sack, shrinking even further until at last he falls into astronomical space and finds himself shrinking down to the surface of a world, a world with trees and plains like our own—only infinitely small!

What do they find in that microcosmic world? The same things Cummings' heroes will find in voyages to other planets, to the bottom of the sea, or to infinite largeness—a maiden to be rescued, a villain to be foiled, a good action-adventure derring-do novel. Kingdoms and republics, Napoleons and scientists, some weird animals, some fantastic cities, but always perfectly comprehensible people.

He utilized the size-changing chemicals in exploring the vaster universe, the macrocosm. Here his hero, in a space ship that grows in size rather than moves in space, grows vaster and vaster until the sun and its planets are reduced to microscopic size and the galaxies and the billions of stars too are but molecules in a universe whose relation to us is that of ourselves to the micro-cosmic. And what happens then? I recall two variations. One is that the Greater Universe is like ours—a planet with people and heroes and villains and a maiden to be rescued. The other is more intriguingly mechanistic—our hero finds himself on the inside of a huge shell, the shell which encircles our universe as an eggshell holds its contents. And what lives on that inner shell of the universe? You guessed it. A maiden to be rescued!

They don't write that story any more either. The concept of the microcosmic world has been dashed to pieces by the discovery of more things than electrons and protons. We now believe we have discovered how many other energy particles of the microcosm? Twenty, is it? Or more? Bodies charged with every variety of energy or not charged at all. The molecule becomes not a simple matter but a vastly complex interweaving of many energies and many particles in many many motions. Nobody today would describe the microcosmic universe as another solar system or dare to invent a voyage into it!

As for the question of the macrocosmic—is this universe indeed a particle or a molecule in some vaster universe? Who can say? Some stories hint at it or touch upon it, suggest, but do not define, for the realization of the complexity, of the ever-changing nature of existence and the impermanence of any state of being has erased the adventuresome ignorance of the days of Ray Cummings.

Certainly we do not expect to find a maiden in distress or a villain to be foiled. I see in Ray Cummings the culmination of the science-fiction story of the mechanistic nineteenth century and the beginning of the adventure story which formed the body of present-day fiction.

He completed Verne's work. He did not venture into sociology. He did not upset one's equilibrium with social prediction. His was the old Sense of Wonder played out in full.

Curiously enough, Cummings still has reader attraction. There is a trend—and has always been—to enjoy stories of derring-do in fantastic settings. This is the stuff of Edgar Rice Burroughs. I have reprinted many Cummings novels in new editions in paperbacks for Ace Books, and they have sold well and have been rewarded by the letters of young readers and nostalgic old-timers with cries of appreciation.

Never mind that their science is antiquated—there are no lost cities in well-explored Africa and no such creatures as Tarzan's anthropoid apes, but Tarzan is a permanent fixture of the world of imagination. The world of science-fiction reading has wide margins and readers are tolerant of the lack of credibility. Enough that they were credible once, that once these things seemed logical; if the storytelling is still exciting, let's read them anyway, accrediting them perhaps as fantasy—we accept them as credible because we wish to do so, not because we are any longer convinced.

What, then, of Edgar Rice Burroughs? He, too, came out of the same period that produced Ray Cummings. His stories of wonder adventure have made their mark in the world. Tarzan is a word to be found in dictionaries and is known to all languages and all lands. Tarzan himself—well, we can believe or disbelieve—but the bulk of his adventures were instances of an almost extinct branch of science fiction—the Imaginary Voyage to a lost race. There is a formula detectable in many Tarzan adventures: he finds a valley or an isolated land in which are lost people: Romans, ant-sized men, tailed men, lost Atlanteans, and so on, all forgotten by our civilization. Usually they have split into two warring factions and Tarzan inevitably gets mixed up with one side or the other. The lost-race story belongs to the roots of science fiction, it is one with Gulliver, and Burroughs makes it live to this very day.

But whereas Cummings eschewed social satire, Burroughs often indulged in it, and many of his novels are enhanced by his deliberate satirical presentation of one or another philosophy. He pokes fun at staid religion in his attack on the blond-wigged priests of Mars ("Help Stamp Out Therns" is a slogan I have seen carried about by fans at more than one convention!); he satirizes Nazism and Communism in his stories of Venus; he builds a parallel with the Earth of World War II in one of his last novels, that of *Beyond the Farthest Star;* he weaves a picture of the miseries of the conquered in *The Moon Men.* Yet his social satire was irrelevant to his popularity. It was his talent in producing wonderful adventure, of building good against evil that prevails.

Burroughs was not a very grand philosopher. His views were pretty much those of the more open-minded American middle class of this century, which were generally speaking good views indeed. He was no Utopian. He did not venture into deep science or propose grandiose schemes for social development. He sought to entertain and in so doing created marvels that caught the mind of the world and still do.

I said something about good against evil just then. I will get back to this by and by. It counts. It's old-fashioned these days but it counts. It cannot be subtracted from the reasons why Burroughs sells today as well as he ever did. Tarzan is good, always good. His foes may be mixed, but his main foes are evil, plain downright evil.

We don't get much of that in mainstream fiction these days. Too bad.

When I hear that millions of young people are reading Burroughs and enjoying him, I rejoice. It may not be brilliant science fiction, but there is a light of hope here that outshines all the sour statistics of youth gone wrong.

Burroughs had his imitators in the twenties and thirties of the *Argosy* and *Blue Book* days of science fiction. Chief among them were Otis Adelbert Kline and Ralph Milne Farley. Farley produced a series of adventure novels laid on Venus which embodied the currently exciting premises of radio—and his novels were *The Radio Planet* series. Good in themselves, they have faded away as imitations always do. Otis Adelbert Kline entered the lists with another Venus-based series of adventure novels done in a very Burroughs style. But what Burroughs had, Kline did not have in more than a mirrorlike fashion. Grand adventure, which has had its followers when reprinted (as I have done in the sixties), but, again, imitation without innovation must always remain shadowed by the work of the imitated.

6

Headquarters: Canopus

AND THEN CAME Edmond Hamilton. In the pages of a ghost-story magazine called *Weird Tales* appeared a group of novelettes of the world in danger. Science fiction from a weird story source, but science fiction back when there was but one such magazine, *Amazing Stories,* and that mainly reprint. Out of the twenties into the early thirties came Hamilton—and a sudden spark that was momentarily to light up the greatest concept of the world of science-fiction ideas: the galactic civilization.

That spark was the Interstellar Patrol. Corn, pure corn. A style marked by endless exclamation points, a gosh-wow-golly type of writing, our side against theirs plotting, a last-minute rush to the lever that alone would save or destroy the day, and a bang ending leaving everyone breathless. No characterization at all—everything strictly cardboard, and the universe very mechanistic too. And yet—the Interstellar Patrol was the crude tiny spark that hinted at what this is all about.

Modern science fiction is delineated by the farthest boundaries of time and space. And the galactic civilization is the turning point of this universe building. A civilization of intelligent beings,

in contact with each other, trading with each other, banded together in some sort of Federation of the Stars to assist, to en-
lighten, to defend. It implies a lot—oh, how much it implies!

There it was in those crude wild formula stories of Edmond
Hamilton in the lurid pages of *Weird Tales* in 1929 and 1930.
The Interstellar Patrol.

Ten thousand years from now? Apparently, a patrol ship of
the stars traveling many hundreds of times the speed of light.
And crewed by one being each of a dozen or two dozen intelligent cooperating civilized worlds, members of the Interstellar
Federation whose headquarters were on a planet of the mighty
sun Canopus. One man from Earth—and the rest of the crew
equals, described as fishmen, snakemen, bearmen, and beings of
weirder stripe, one each from many stars. All working together
as a trained crew to rescue stars from danger, to fight off invaders
from other galaxies, to beat down natural disasters that would
threaten the civilized worlds. Galactic civilization!

Hamilton told us little of this civilization. He never explained
how ships could travel at such speeds, relying on the passage of
ten thousand years of scientific progress to make that reasonable.
He stated for granted an exchange of cultures but never depicted
it. Cardboard does not allow any great depth of character or
vision of background. But the idea, the idea!

Galactic civilization. It imples going to the moon, going to
Mars and the other planets. It implies colonizing where colonizing is possible. It implies the multiplicity of worlds and the intellectual kinship of intelligent beings whatever their form. If
we think, therefore we are brothers. It implies mankind covering
the space between the stars. It implies making that travel sufficiently practical so that commerce between stars becomes practical, commonplace. It implies civilizations taking from each other
what is desirable, presumably what is best for each. It implies
an end to boundaries and the acceptance of infinite future and
infinite progress outward in the universe.

It implies so much. There it was, hot on the heels of Verne
and Wells and Cummings. A new young writer then, Edmond
Hamilton, with the spark that lit the infinite. Hamilton is still
writing, he is far more sophisticated, far more able and skilled

a storyteller than the youth who pounded out those tales of the Patrol, but he surely cannot hope to surpass that concept which for one moment pushed the borders of science fiction ahead.

7

The Supreme Moment of the Cosmos

THAT WAS 1929. In 1930 there appeared in England (in the U.S.A. in 1931) another writer whose work was to further advance science fiction into the modern era and who was to present a vision of futurity so vast that none have ever sucessfully tried to duplicate it. This was W. Olaf Stapledon, and the book was called *Last and First Men*.

Last and First Men came out of the blue. Nobody had ever heard of Stapledon before, he had written no short stories for the magazines and he had apparently read little or nothing of the material that had influenced the small world of science-fiction readers. But what he came up with was a seemingly endless treasure chest of concepts and ideas which he had worked out by himself and which came forth like an explosion of wonders that threatened to transmute all thinking thereafter. What *Last and First Men* was, was nothing less than the entire history of humanity from the twentieth century to the end of the Last Men on the planet Neptune two billion years from now!

It is a magnificent book, an inspiring one. Beginning in detail, Stapledon traces the coming centuries—and this is his major weak point. For already this is out of date; trying to foretell the exact political moves of a mere twenty years must always defeat the prophet. It is easier to predict on the basis of thousands of years. So it is with Stapledon, but none have predicted as he has done.

To skip the earliest centuries, what we have is the history of eighteen species of humanity, of which ours is but the First. Each species spans tens of thousands and in some cases millions of years of history and each species has its philosophical and social problems, which inevitably bring about its downfall until the next evolutionary level of humanity evolves, takes charge of the world, and starts off again. Stapledon sees humanity as a soaring spirit, always trying, never quite succeeding in conquering the limitations of flesh and body. Advance after advance leads but to setback after setback as the universe proves to be beyond the total grasp of man's efforts. But the efforts are ever more magnificent, ever more challenging, and mankind gives the universe a great fight before it ends its struggle.

Stapledon did not believe that star flight would ever come about nor that space flight would ever prove very practical or produce any special favor for mankind. The only other intelligence man was to encounter was on Mars and the result of the war against this virus-like, utterly alien intelligence was to ruin both worlds for hundreds of thousands of years. Mankind eventually was to find and contact intelligences on other star systems, but never visit them in person. Humanity changes worlds twice. When planetary disaster overtakes the Fifth Men a few hundred million years from now, the race emigrates to Venus, by then a habitable world. The transition brings about another downfall and further evolutions; a billion years from now humanity moves to Neptune, where it finally dies out with the Eighteenth and greatest species.

The task of outlining each species, of showing advance on a scale of millions of years, should prove beyond any mortal writer's capability, but Stapledon managed to achieve it. His approach is philosophical, his philosophy is Wellsian and mystical, his patience endless, and his faith in mankind clearly unbreakable. His Neptunian men are very nearly godlike, but they are not gods. Stapledon sees advanced mankind as achieving a state of universal harmony so integrated as to create an overmind common to all. The racial mind becomes the thinking single spirit of all men and it is this mass mind, the combined brain power of millions of individuals free of the mud and muck that so bog down the First Men of our own day, that enables the Last Men to contact similar racial minds throughout the universe. The Last Men begin to envision the whole of existence and to possess, for at least a brief moment, the kind of omniscience that we would ascribe only to God.

When science-fiction readers had begun to absorb the shock of this vast opening up of futurity, Stapledon was ready with his next and greatest concept, the book entitled *Star Maker*. This is the history of the cosmos itself. It spans all of time from beginning to end. It encompasses the universes of primitive natural laws before our own and it suggests those universes that are to come after our universe disappears. In the main *Star Maker* deals with our own cosmos, with the rise of intelligence in the universe, with the development of that union of racial minds which becomes the galactic mind, and continues to that union of galactic minds which becomes for one infinite moment the universal mind, the instant which Stapledon calls the Supreme Moment of the Cosmos.

But with compassion and skill Stapledon does not throw all of this at us in one long lecture. He starts with a single human being, disillusioned, bitter, seeking the meaning of everything. This becomes the disembodied mind which soars forth first to probe the past and learn of an Earth which existed millions of years before us and faced similar problems and of its demise. Then to explore other worlds of intelligent beings (and what a variety and what wonders!). Then to witness in one chapter all that was detailed in the nearly four hundred pages of *Last and First Men*. Then on to the development of successful racial minds that did bridge the cosmos, that did manage to solve what humanity was never to solve. So on, until solar minds became galactic minds and that supreme moment. Then the slow path downward to the extinction and burning out of this galaxy and its companion galaxies. The detailed section of the rise and fall of this, our own, universe covers about a hundred billion years.

Reading the book is an experience. Is it possible to read it without being moved? Without being in some way philosophically affected? I think not. It transmuted my thinking certainly. From Wells to Cummings, add Burroughs, add others, it is Stapledon who probably instilled in me a faith in humanity I cannot wholly lose, depressed as I may become at various times with the vicissitudes of the world.

But what was its effect on science fiction? Unfortunately not as great as it should have been, for one prime reason, I suspect. While *Last and First Men* was published in America early enough to be known, it did not deal with atomic power, it did not believe in interplanetary flight, and its immediate political predictions were not convincing. *Star Maker*, which would have had a far greater impact, was not published in the United States until long after World War II. A few fans and a few writers secured the British edition, published in 1937 by Methuen, but not enough to influence what had become the main source of science-fiction conjecture, the American pulp magazines of the thirties and forties.

For me *Star Maker* acted to establish in my mind what must be termed the cosmic vision. Hamilton had spoken of ten thousand years and interstellar confederation. Stapledon spoke of the galactic unity of all intelligent minds when confronted by the enigma of the origin and destiny of existence itself—for any discussion of the whys and wherefores of the universe must ultimately be a discussion of the meaning of being and understanding. Stapledon was a mystic who based his mysticism not on mumbo jumbo, primitive omens, or the accidental configuration of the zodiac, but on the most wide-lensed view of the astronomical and biological sciences themselves.

He was not an atheist. It is not possible to read Stapledon and to see what he sees in humanity and the meaning of intelligent striving and yet view cold atheism as having much point. He is not an advocate of religion either, for that, too, seems too simple, too primitive a solution. But he is a profound believer in what one would call cosmic unity. Existence *is,* therefore existence must have meaning beyond any single mortal life.

Or, as the last of the Last Men says, two billion years from now as his race dies on Neptune: "Great are the stars, and man is of no account to them. But man is a fair spirit, whom a star conceived and a star kills. He is greater than those bright blind companies. For though in them there is incalculable potentiality, in him there is achievement, small but actual. . . . Man was winged hopefully. He had in him to go further than this short flight, now ending. He proposed even that he should become the

Flower of All Things, and that he should learn to be the All-Knowing, the All-Admiring. . . ."

But the rise of modern science fiction was not to benefit from the farther vision of *Star Maker* since that was a vision withheld from the makers of science fiction at a time when it would have done the most good. *Star Maker* was not a successful book, as far as I can see. I do not think it saw a second edition in England. Stapledon wrote other works in the thirties, two of which are masterpieces. One is *Last Men in London,* the account of two people of our own time as seen through the perceptive cosmic vision of a Neptunian Last Man. The other is in my opinion the best effort to predict the oncoming of that species of men who will be to Homo sapiens what we are to Homo Neanderthalensis. This is *Odd John,* a novel of a boy who was born out of humanity and who found a few others like himself. It ends disastrously, for Stapledon continued in the line of his first book —man must strive many times before he succeeds once. But *Odd John* is head and shoulders above other efforts to depict the same thing—the novel of the next higher species of man. (Other instances include *Slan* by A. E. Van Vogt, *The New Adam* by Stanley G. Weinbaum, *The Wonder* by J. D. Beresford, *Childhood's End* by Arthur C. Clarke, and *More than Human* by Theodore Sturgeon.)

Instead of taking off from *Star Maker's* many galactic conceptions, it was not until Isaac Asimov wrote the group of stories that were to be published as the *Foundation* trilogy that the shape of galactic Things to Come was brought into the idea-structure of s-f writing.

8

The Decline and Fall
of the Galactic Empire

IT WAS IN 1942 that the magazine then known as *Astounding Science Fiction* began the first of Isaac Asimov's series of stories which, when completed in 1949, were to become the *Foundation* novels, that series which was voted a Hugo as the "most outstanding science fiction series" of them all. The novels are *Foundation, Foundation and Empire*, and *Second Foundation*. I am inclined to think, in the context of this book, that they are the pivot of modern science fiction.

The stories published before *Foundation* belong to the old line, the stories published after belong to "modern" science fiction.

What did *Foundation* have that was so pivotal?

Nothing less than the analysis and problems to be involved with the Decline and Fall of the Galactic Empire—and its reconstruction. In so doing Asimov clarified much that was implicit in previous science-fictional projections into the wherefore of space travel and what will follow after the stars are first reached. He developed the theme of the rise of a united effort to combine all the colonized worlds under one rule, emanating from Terra Triumphant, as from Rome, and showed the faults and flaws of that unified effort. People had written of planet flight and of star flight, they had written of colonies planted on worlds that circle alien stars, they had described the hazards and perils of travels between the worlds, they had depicted the struggles for exploration, the Magellans and the Cortezes of those interstellar days.

It was left to Asimov to gather the whole together and say, they will make an empire and that empire will have its day, much as Rome, and for much the same reasons will fall as Rome fell. Between barbarians and the rise of local nationalisms there will be a period of chaos, an interstellar Dark Ages, and during that time, that Interregnum, there will arise the many star nations that are to be—the equivalents of France and England and Spain, based upon Rome but not of Rome, holding the reconstruction of Rome as an ideal but never achieving it, for time and science and the growth of mental horizons will make such a second Roman Empire forever an impossibility.

In short, Asimov applied to future history the lessons of past history. He brought to the attention of the science-fiction cosmos the fact that humanity follows patterns and that those patterns, though similar, differ in scope, differ in intensity and internal nature, that the rise of civilization follows a spiral that makes certain events seem to recur predictably but always on a new and vaster level.

The theme of his three great novels is that during the building of an empire of human-colonized worlds there grew up a body of knowledge of human potentials, human activities and historical analysis which became a science by which humanity itself could be directed, predicted, patterned much as chemists know how to organize compounds and create new materials by their knowledge of the actions of the laws of chemistry and physics.

Asimov named this science psychohistory, and in the first book he defines it as "that branch of mathematics which deals with the reactions of human conglomerates to fixed social and economic stimuli. . . . Implicit in all these definitions is the assumption that the human conglomerate being dealt with is sufficiently large for valid statistical treatment. . . . A further necessary assumption is that the human conglomerate be itself unaware of psychohistoric analysis in order that its reactions be truly random."

Students of psychohistory learned to analyze the events of a given social situation and correctly and mathematically to work out the probable results. In short, to predict with a high degree of accuracy, based upon the knowledge of all the variables, just what would happen and how and when it would happen.

This is done today with computers in many fields. To do it with all humanity, to predict accurately the historical events of next year or next century, however, is beyond our capacity at this time simply because in the relatively primitive state of our information there are too many variables, too much that is obscure or unclear about past events, and our science of psychology is still in a formative, conflicting, and anything but exact stage. Economics has not yet been fully accepted as a science —the world still follows several major economic systems—and we do not yet know what balance and proportion of strength to assign to economic motivation, psychological motivation, and environmental motivation—not to mention simple opportunism and "mutant" unpredictables.

In Asimov's novels it is assumed that during the course of the tens of thousands of years of the rise of the Galactic Empire enough data were compiled, enough information was tested, enough science was advanced to make possible a true science of social prediction. This is psychohistory.

The story of the *Foundation* novels, then, is the prediction of the imminent fall of the Empire, of a million worlds cast adrift, as commerce and the exchange of information ceases, as interplanetary wars and piracy and the onslaught of worlds turned barbarian begins the process of smashing up the Empire and reducing it to ruins. To offset this, the leaders of that science establish the Foundation, an institute of monastic devotion dedicated to tracing the course of the fall and to seeking out and assisting those factors which will rapidly bring this Dark Age to an end and restore civilization through the galaxy.

In the course of the three novels Asimov deals with the rise of planets once obscure, with the manipulations of the Foundation's secret operatives thereon, of the maneuvers of politics and psychology needed to shore up the key worlds of the galaxy to come. The second novel deals with the unexpected—the oncoming of a mutant unpredictable, a Charlemagne of galactic history whose brief personal power seemed almost for one shining moment to restore the Empire that had been, only to fall again with the death of the single leader. And the inner problem of the Foundation and its men, which were not immune to psychohistory themselves and against which corruption a secret Second Foundation had been set up—a touch Isaac Asimov alone might have been capable of.

The parallel between all this and the actual past history of Earth should be clear to anyone with any knowledge of history beginning with Rome. We see in the fall of the Empire the fall of Rome and the failure of Roman civilization. We see the efforts of innumerable little pockets throughout Europe to retain what they had learned from Rome, to set up little Romes to offset the barbarian sea around them. We see the dream and vision of restoring the Rome that was, the vision that occupied nations for a thousand years after, the same vision that caused the Kaiser of Germany and the Czar of Russia alike to bear the title of Caesar even down to our own twentieth century.

We have also in the Foundation a parallel of the Church and its monks, keeping the records, binding together the legend of Rome with religious bonds and ties of the mind even though the secular ties had been torn asunder. But we detect also a more modern parallel, that of the latter-day Church, the Communist party which seeks through a set of theories based on the premises of a pseudo psychohistory known as Marxism to predict the movements of human masses and historical change.

For psychohistory is the science that Marxism never became. Marxism, if you are not aware of it, is not just a plan for socialism or a scheme for uprisings—it was put together in the middle of the nineteenth century as allegedly a science of the movement of history. It is taught to this day as a required science in Communist party run countries.

The validity of this Marx-Engels "science" can be shown by the simple fact that after a half century as the official basis of the U.S.S.R., its innumerable students have never successfully predicted anything. Their history proceeds from one ghastly bungle to another, from one costly oversight to another, and their course among nations has been marked with incredible clumsiness, crudity, and a constant jarring departure from the "democracy" and "freedom from want and fear" that their whole crusade was supposed to achieve.

Which should not be surprising. For, while Marxism has a glib logic in its ringing analyses of the nature of society and the operations of economics, these are all nineteenth-century *mechanistic* conceptions. No "Marxist" yet dares to challenge the original premises and state the need for further data, for the inclusion of psychological information, and for further study of the not-so-simple problems of economics. Marxism predates psychology itself—and it has never yet taken even that body of information into account!

What we have is the equivalent of a man who reads the first two or three chapters of an elementary first textbook of chemistry —and immediately sets himself up as a working chemist!

I conjecture that Asimov took this basic premise of Marx and Engels, said to himself that there was a point there—that the movements of the human mass must be subject to the laws of motion and interraction, and that a science could be developed based upon mathematics and utilizing all the known data— millions and millions of variables certainly!—that would be what Marxism thought it was and never could be.

This was psychohistory. By the twelve thousandth year of the Galactic Era it was almost an exact science.

In the Foundation novels, the work of the psychohistorians succeeds. The predicted thirty thousand years of barbarism is averted and the loss of knowledge and lapse of planets into savagery is averted.

But because science fiction builds upon science fiction and one man's originations become the next man's accepted premises, the rise, reign, and fall of a galactic empire is now taken for granted in many millennia-spanning novels to come after. Not always is the galaxy restored—that particular plot belongs to Asimov. More often we have novels of adventure during the tens of thousands of years after the fall, on worlds which have forgotten their common ancestry and common heritage with Earth and other stars. Humanity is found on a million worlds on a million levels of culture from cave man to high technology— and the Galactic Empire and Earth itself are either legends, religious allegories, or altogether forgotten.

Then we have novels and stories which take place during the restoration—on a higher scale—of contact between the myriad human worlds of the universe. We begin to approach the Stapledon theme of a harmony of intelligences that covers the universe.

9

The Cosmogony of the Future

WHAT THE FOUNDATION SERIES did was to create the point of departure for the full cosmogony of science-fiction future history. It is possible to analyze present-day stories and place them into that framework of millions of years to come. We can establish a pattern of premises accepted without acknowledgment. We can tell what is implied by the simple facts of a story's background.

Are the science-fiction writers wrong in utilizing a framework which is subject to such close definition? Not really. There is only a limited number of general possibilities open to human conjecture. When all the many highly inventive minds of science-fiction writers find themselves falling again and again into similar patterns, we must perforce say that this does seem to be what all our mental computers state as the shape of the future.

What, then, is this history?

First, we have the initial voyages to the moon and to the planets of our Solar System. In this sequence we also include stories of the contact of man with intelligent species elsewhere in this system—Martians, Jovians, Venusians, if any. Stories of the first efforts to set up terrestrial bases on such planets. Stories of the first colonies of such worlds, their problems internal and external, their conflicts with the parent world, their breakaway or interplanetary commerce, spaceship trade lanes, space pirates, asteroid mining, the weird wonders of the Outer Planets, and so forth.

Second, the first flights to the stars. The problem of whether science can ever exceed the speed of light—a very important one where the problem of colonization is concerned. Starships, ships that must travel centuries and contain generations descended from the original crews. Other planets of other stars. Intelligences on such planets and our problems with them or against them. Human colonies on other starry systems. Contact with Mother Earth, independence or dependence. Commerce—exploitation or otherwise.

Third, the Rise of the Galactic Empire. The rise of contact and commerce between many human-colonized worlds or many worlds of alien intelligences that have come to trust and do business with one another. The problem of mutual relations and the solution, usually in the form of treaties or defensive alliances. Implacable aliens in the cosmos who must be fought. The need for defense. The rise of industrial or financial or political powers, the eventual triumph of one and the establishment of a federation, a union, an alliance, or an autocratic empire of worlds, dominated usually from Old Earth.

Fourth, the Galactic Empire in full bloom, regardless of what form it takes. Commerce between worlds an established fact, and adventures while dealing with worlds in and out of the Empire. The farthest planets, those of the Galactic Rim, considered as mavericks. The problem of aliens again outside the Empire, and outside our own galaxy. Politics within the government setup, intrigues, and dynasties, robotic mentalities versus human mentalities. "Terra-forming" worlds for colonization. The exploration of the rest of the galaxy by official exploration ships, or adventurers, or commercial pioneers.

Fifth, the Decline and Fall of the Galactic Empire. Intrigue and palace revolt. Breakaway planets. The alliance of worlds strained beyond its limits by rebellion, alien wars, corruption, scientific inability to keep up with internal or external problems. The rise of restless subject worlds. Decline, then loss of contact with farthest worlds, crumbling of commerce, failure of space lanes, distrust, finally worlds withdrawing into themselves as the empire/alliance/federation/union becomes an empty shell or is destroyed at its heart.

Sixth, the Interregnum. Worlds reverting to prespace-flight conditions, savagery, barbarism, primitive forms of life, superstition. Worlds taking to barbarian raids on defenseless isolated planets, hastening the downfall of knowledge. Fragments of space flight, fragments of empire, some starships, some efforts to revive. Thousands of years of loss of contact. Humanity in this period becomes indigenous to most of the habitable planets of the galaxy, forgetting origins. Evolutionary changes may take place. Alterations of form to fit differing world conditions—giant men, tiny men, water-dwelling men, flying men, mutations.

Seventh, the Rise of a Permanent Galactic Civilization. The restoration of commerce between worlds. The reexploration of lost and uncontacted worlds and the bringing them back to high-technology, democratic levels. The efforts to establish trade between human worlds that no longer seem kin. Beating down new efforts to form empires, efforts which sometimes succeed and revert to approximations of the previous period, with similar results. Eventual rise of galactic harmony among intelligences. The exploration of other galaxies and of the entire universe.

Eighth, the Challenge to God. Galactic harmony and an un-dreamed-of high level of knowledge leads to experiments in creation, to harmony between galactic clusters, and possible exploration of the other dimensions of existence. The effort to match Creation and to solve the last secrets of the universe. Sometimes seeking out and confronting the Creative Force or Being or God itself, sometimes merging with that Creative First Premise. The end of the universe, the end of time, the beginning of a new universe or a new time-space continuum.

All the above and every variation on it—that's the scope of modern science fiction today.

And when some well-intentioned reporter or radio commentator calls up a science-fiction writer at the time of Apollo and asks, "Now that men have landed on the moon what will you write about?" is it so strange that he is answered with a shrug and a smile of forgiveness?

10

Of Men Like Gods

WHEN I THINK of stories that have to do with challenging God or becoming God or having a hero of godlike powers I have to think of A. E. Van Vogt. For one of Van Vogt's abiding characteristics is to make his heroes so invulnerable, so omniscient, so gifted with superhuman powers as to encourage the suspicion that his heroes are all really God in disguise.

Van Vogt is a universe maker by instinct. From the first his stories have concerned themselves with extraordinary powers, with new concepts in science or in mental gymnastics, and he constantly seems to strive to create new systems of thought and mental order which will permit the creation of supermen. It is not an accident that his first fame-making novel was *The World of Null-A*, which presumed to be an exposition of the General Semantics of Alfred Korzybski, a philosophy of semantics which was thought to be the key to truly scientific and accurate communication between men. It was a Depression gimmick idea, one of the many that sprouted in those unhappy, desperate times. Its premise was that if we could only understand each other *perfectly* we could end wars, miseries, and so on. Everything that was bad about society was due to lack of perfect comprehension of each other's words and writings. The theory of General Semantics postulated a new form of mind training designed to eliminate emotional coloration from all communications and thinking.

Actually it was never clear just what *The World of Null-A* had to do with the real General Semantics, save for the use of interesting quotations before each chapter. Van Vogt's hero turned out to be rather similar to God. Gifted by powers of clear thinking and identical mental conceptions with others trained in the mental techniques, he was virtually uncatchable. In fact he could not truly be killed. Trapped, cornered, slain, he turned up instantly elsewhere safe and whole again! General Semantics, according to Van Vogt, supplied this godlike re-creating.

That book, whose action took place in a future of the period between the interplanetary and interstellar phases, was followed by Van Vogt's effort to create a godlike being, this time by evolutionary means. It was *Slan,* with the same premise as *Odd John,* but this time presenting not an abortive immature superman, but a whole race of supermen, fighting for their place against prejudice and having a tough time of it. The book's protagonist, Jommy Cross, is a boy of *slan* roots, running from his oppressors in a fear-ridden city of the future. But *slans* are supermen, though not gods, and in some ways *Slan* is one of Van Vogt's most successful books.

Van Vogt himself is a perpetual seeker after mental godhood. Van Vogt is a talented writer who utilizes his novels to propel many novel schools of thought, making them move with dramatic skill, a talent that calls for a toboggan technique of plotting which, as he once described it, required inserting a new idea every seven hundred words!

A devastating criticism was made of his work by Damon Knight in his book *In Search of Wonder,* the sort of breakdown of Van Vogt's plots to show their inconsistencies, their flaws of characterization and plot. It was the sort of jugular dissection that Mark Twain made of the work of James Fenimore Cooper—and with much the same result: nothing. Van Vogt is still among the two or three best-selling authors of science fiction in America. Whatever may be said of his plotting, he is always read compellingly, he is fascinating, and one gains a sensation of having had one's brain exercised.

I find Van Vogt always unusual. No two works of his are ever quite alike and no one can possibly tell in advance each new twist of the toboggan slide. He embodies all the phases of the cosmic future. His stories span all time and all space.

The Galactic Empire in full bloom is, for instance, the scene of two of his best novels, *The Weapon Makers* and *The Weapon Shops of Isher.* Here in the year 4784, the Empire is at its height, the Empress Innelda of the Isher dynasty is the titular ruler of the universe. But nothing is ever taken for granted in a Van

Vogt novel. Here we have a counterforce to Isher in the form of the mysterious—and "Godlike"!—guild of the Weapon Shops. Possessed of certain scientific achievements denied to the Imperial forces, the weapon shops are not openly in rebellion, possibly may not even want rebellions. What they are is a guarantee of personal liberty even amidst the dictatorship of an empire that spans the stars. Their trick—the sale of weapons to individuals—their slogan, "The right to buy weapons is the right to be free." The National Rifle Association and the gun lobby should jump for joy with such a slogan—and Van Vogt had it more than twenty-five years ago!

Just how applicable this revolutionary slogan is is a matter of the time and the place. It was written into the United States Constitution. It is under attack right now. It, the privilege of owning personal weapons, is denied in all totalitarian and dictatorial countries. But it is not a simple proposition. It has ramifications and Van Vogt is aware of them. Once again his hero is to all intents and purposes God, himself impregnable and aided by a person who swings forever between five million years in the past and five million years in the future!

In *The Voyage of the Space Beagle,* we have a Van Vogt novel of phase two, the first explorations of the stars—and also an explosion of another science of the mind, Nexialism. The *Space Beagle* set out simply to explore the many planets of the nearby stars, it ends heading out toward a galaxy 900 million light years away in order to exhaust and shake off an almost godlike antagonist which nevertheless had met its masters in the human beings who were masters of Nexial thinking.

The Mixed Men is another interstellar epic, this time belonging to the Galactic Empire phase, wherein an Imperial ship encounters a hideout group of planet colonies. And *The War Against the Rull* is an intergalactic combat epic which must be taking place during the seventh phase of the future, for the galaxy is united and only an intelligence from outside this star cloud can break up its unity.

Van Vogt swings back and forth, like his victim of Isher, making all time and space his field, and showing in innumerable ways that man is equal to the greatest potential and is godlike

in himself. Man may vary—he may advance himself by conquest
of his own mind or by evolutionary development of the next
race, or he may deliberately remake himself into a scientifically
constructed superior form, as in the recent Van Vogt novel *The
Silkie*, whose hero is a being of that classification, able to change
shape at will, able to be a space ship and a submarine, able to
think with computerlike capacity and speed, able to play God
as far as the old-style humans were concerned.

To the uninitiated layman all this may smell of megalomania
and perhaps paranoia, but Van Vogt remains atop the lists of
the most favored and best-selling science-fiction writers. There
must be a reason and that reason is as I have outlined before:
he has an instinctual belief in humanity, he believes in the in-
vincibility of humanity, he refuses to accept boundaries of time
and space.

The fact is that science-fiction readers agree with him. They,
too, cannot believe that humanity has limitations.

Call it megalomania, if you will. There is indeed a megalo-
maniac element to most s-f novels. Whereas mystery novels deal
with the saving of a single being, or the avenging of a single
injustice, and western novels likewise, whereas war novels and
spy novels may deal with the fate of cities or armies or nations,
an incredible percentage of science-fiction thrillers will settle
for nothing less than the fate of the entire world, or some
other planet, or the Galactic Empire, or the whole of mankind,
or even occasionally the entire universe. Read through the
blurbs of a hundred paperback s-f books and count how many
have at stake not just the hero's life but a cause of planetary
vastness. Science-fiction writers are not just universe makers,
they are also universe savers.

Perhaps their vision, wide-lensed and far-ranging, is right.
Perhaps in this century and at *this time* of this century it *is*
actually the world that is at stake or all humanity—and only
science and the defenders of science can save it.

A darned near unanswerable case can be made for their being
right. If so, megalomania is not accidental.

It may also explain why this type of cosmos-spanning novel
came into full bloom only after the end of World War II.

Science fiction does not merely build upon previous science fiction—it also projects answers to the crises of the day, it builds upon the immediate present, no matter how far-flung the field of the novel.

But before we get into the matter of the very pivotal problems of the last third of the twentieth century, let us have a look at a universe maker who has been doing exactly that. I refer to Philip José Farmer and his novels of the Lord Creator Jadawin.

11

Of Gods Like Men

FARMER IS BEST KNOWN and most often referred to in critical works about science fiction as the first to introduce speculation about sex intelligently as a legitimate subject of science-fiction extrapolation. I would discuss that here too save that it has been done too often and it is not my intent to depart from what I consider to be the main drive shafts of science fiction.

Farmer's brilliant novel *The Lovers,* and such books of his as *Flesh* and *Strange Relations,* have all been analyzed and exclaimed over before. They can be fitted into the framework I have outlined but what interests me is the premise behind his most recent series, all paperback originals: *The Maker of Universes, The Gates of Creation, A Private Cosmos,* and *Behind the Walls of Terra.* For, although writers like Stapledon have speculated on humanity's rising to the point where it could compete with God, we have in these stories the premise that a physical species, akin to man in every way (emotionally and physically), had advanced its civilization and control of the secrets of nature so far that it was able to create entire universes, closed cosmoses, establish whatever arbitrary laws of "science" it wished to govern these man-made continuums, and then use them for its own private playgrounds!

The idea is the implied one behind any religious dogma of

creation. God the Creator who made the skies and the earth as outlined in the Book of Genesis never defines His motives. God established the world as He saw fit to establish it, made animals and beasts, created water and land, set the rules for night and day, and presumably laid down all the laws of nature at that time. What was His motive? We can only assume it was self-satisfaction of some sort. Surely the restrictions laid down on man, as He created him according to the Bible, imply that. The need for praising the Lord, for doing His work, and so forth, all in the various divine ordinances, would indicate that God made this universe for His own pleasure or for His own experimentation for some purpose we cannot suspect.

Take this basic premise of religion, then establish the belief that science, if carried on at its rate of progress as of this century, must inevitably uncover all the secrets of the universe, and does it not imply that mankind, so armed and so learned, can then also create self-sustained, closed-circle private cosmoses, out of our own space and time, but accessible to the builder and obeying under stress whatever whimsical laws an artificial physics and arbitrary biology or chemistry will set up? Stapledon, ultimately mystical, did not feel that mankind or even the galactic mass intelligence would be able to do more than glimpse the Face of the Creator. Less mystical, modern s-f writers are coming around to the idea that, given enough time (centuries, millennia, millions of years) and sufficient data (all that there is to know), our descendants can duplicate to their own design anything at all.

Such are the capacities of the race Phil Farmer calls the Lords. They reached a point where each made his own universe to crown his own glory. Into one of these plunged the man Wolff, from our own day, and found himself in a world of tiers, not spherical, not moving through the skies like our planets, but a flat world, with level laid upon level, like a Babylonian ziggurat, until at the top level is the house of the Lord (who turns out to be Wolff himself, whose real name is Jadawin). On each level there is a different type of civilization—all more or less related to our own world's past histories and legendry—for it would appear that Jadawin has some relationship with the universe in which this our earth exists (which we begin to suspect is also the creation of one of the band of Lords).

The Maker of Universes and its sequels are not grand cosmological epics—they are action-adventure novels, with danger and challenge à la Edgar Rice Burroughs and Sir Walter Scott. The idea is there and the mind-challenging concepts are implicit. We read, as the series goes on, of other universes and other Lords (Farmer makes it a postulate that all Lords distrust each other and are forever trying to trap and destroy each other), and the variety is awe-inspiring and constantly surprising. The novels are a veritable fireworks of new concepts in biology and fantasy lands—the creations fall over each other and the possibilities continue to burst from Farmer's mind in ever-growing array.

Farmer's pocket universes just would not have been possible to the science-fiction writers of the pre-Foundation days. They would not have been possible ten years ago. They are possible today because of the advanced state of the art, because science-fiction readers have become aware of the cosmological implications of man's progress, and because also the past few years have shucked off the fear of religious bigotry that would have inhibited writers and publishers (more the publishers than the writers, I must admit) only a short time ago.

Any religious person—God-fearing would be the right word—would presumably object to such sacrilegious ideas as that man could ever compete directly with God. The implication that God Himself might be just another mortal playing at scientific games would cause a true believer to write furious letters to publishers. But this no longer happens. Apparently science fiction no longer needs to fear the anger of the believers.

I am reminded of one of the classics of the preatomic days, C. S. Lewis' brilliant novel *Out of the Silent Planet*. This was the first of a trilogy intended as an allegorical depiction of the conflict between materialistic science and moralistic theology. The second and third novels, *Perelandra* and *That Hideous Strength*, cannot be classified as science fiction, the second being almost straight fantasy and the third primarily a thriller-suspense novel. But *Out of the Silent Planet*, with its trip to Mars, its unforgettable depiction of the three intelligent yet dissimilar races of Martians, is indeed science fiction. But science fiction with a moral—which is that a high civilization must be God-fearing and adhere to the conviction that there is a Higher Morality above that of mortal lawmaking.

Out of the Silent Planet survives as a classic on the sheer literary talent of its author, a colleague of J. R. R. Tolkien. But its message has gained no adherents in the modern writings of the field and indeed its philosophy strikes today's readers as painfully dated.

I can only ascribe this to the growing social, moral, and political crisis of our times—the crisis that started with the first test firing of the first atomic bomb and has been growing ever since. The national controversy of a few years ago as to whether or not "God is dead" is evidence of this. Such a shocking concept would not have got to first base before World War II. But in our time it became a subject that could be discussed—and sometimes accepted—in the pulpits of churches themselves.

Science-fiction writers were a little slow to recognize the implications of this debate, but the Farmer novels are an indication that as a result of it all barriers are down when the discussion of the creation of the universe and of mankind is concerned. God as a physical real being is now a valid subject for science-fictional speculation. The universe *did* start—that would seem to be a fact. How and why and when and whodunit are therefore valid speculative themes for the s-f writer.

Astronomically, the time of the apparent origin of the universe has been established and current theory seems to settle mainly on a Big Bang several billion years ago—wherein a single giant atom burst and the result is what we see about us—the parts of which are still speeding away from the scene of the explosion. All very well. It still begs the question of where did the single Primal Atom come from and what was there before it and why did it go off?

Science merely moves God a bit farther into the distance, but the human mind is not capable of the concept of personal non-existence. It is beyond our computer capacity, that's all. Hence we refuse to discuss that very primitive question of the very, very young, "Who created God?"

S-f writers can't answer that either—they must beg the question even as Farmer does. But they can and do bring a physical God right into their stories if they see a plot angle to it.

What's more they get no kickback from doing so. I have published novels such as Dean Koontz's *Fear That Man,* wherein God is depicted as an evil force and is at one point turned into a small worm and *stepped on!* I got no protests from readers. My publisher received no letters of indignation from the religious. A dozen years ago such a reference would have raised a storm. Not so any more. We live in troubled times and the old standards are dissolving.

12

Three Barriers to Futurity

HOWEVER, a vengeful God may have the last laugh yet. We are faced with three crises of the last section of the twentieth century which may yet send us all to hell. These are hurdles that the writers of science fiction must face and overcome if they are convincingly to depict any future for humanity, either here or in the stars, in the twenty-first century and those to follow.

They are the hurdles of pollution, overpopulation, and the Bomb.

I do not think that any science-fiction novel purporting to deal with the next two or three centuries can be acceptable without in some way mentioning how the author sees the solution of these problems. For stories laid a thousand or more years in the future we can assume that whatever scars will result from this century will have been alleviated by time—mutations excepted, of course. But the modern s-f writer must clear these three hurdles to make any post-twentieth-century scene credible.

The fact is that not all of them do. It is easier to ignore them, to write a story taking place in London or New York or Luna

City or Marsopolis a hundred or so years from now and treat the background as if the population of the world were just the same, as if merely the addition of a few fancy gadgets, trick language, and so on would make it acceptable as a future setting. That is bad thinking. It is hack writing. If we are dealing with something written twenty years ago, or in Ray Cummings' day, sure. We understand. But now?

Of the three problems, the Bomb has been with us since 1945. Overpopulation and pollution are recent—we have really become aware of their menace only in the past two or three years, though scientists and conservationists have been warning us for much longer than that. But they are coming to the fore now, more and more acutely every day.

Pollution is the least of the three. You scarcely find it mentioned in s-f stories, except in combination with overpopulation. I cannot at this moment think of a single novel in which pollution specifically and alone is the primary basis of the story. Oh, there are short stories and novelettes and probably novels wherein the characters, as a matter of ordinary everyday usage, carry around respirators and put them on before venturing into the streets or open air. Such stories are laid in the next hundred years. I recall tales wherein everyone wears outdoor coveralls and gloves—but these may also be radiation foils and perhaps not quite related to pollution per se.

Pollution is on the public conscience these days and, of the three problems, it seems to be the one that may very likely be taken care of properly in the next dozen years. In this respect, maybe s-f writers are correct in not assigning it cardinal importance. We have indeed polluted rivers, and the air above our cities is heavy with smog, and the countryside a grayed-out mess.

And nobody has to say anything about the increasingly bad taste of water, nor the dirt that clings to windshields and other objects.

But things are being done. The fact is that government has awakened to the matter and more and more cities are taking steps to limit pollution and contamination. In the way that governments and profit-making corporations do things, it isn't being rushed, but it is being done. Work is going on about the introduction of automobile engines of a nonpolluting type. Electric batteries will be coming back for running cars. Not overnight, but probably in time to permit some recovery. We may save a redwood or two by the time Congress gets around to it. Nobody has a good word to say for pollution, so politicians can safely support the fight against it. As for private interests, eventually they will see the light too.

I do not think pollution is a problem in itself. In connection with overpopulation, it is. It may be that, with the geometric progression of the world's population, the fight against pollution may prove to be one against an enemy growing even as we combat it. Overpopulation is going to be the hellish problem of the next ten to twenty years. If we do nothing now, by that time it will be too late. With twenty years more of the present rate of increase, the problem of overpopulation will begin to merge with the problem of the Bomb.

Science fiction has not done too well with overpopulation by itself either. It has come up but lately. Still it was foreshadowed. There were classics of the pre-forties that spoke of worlds so populated that they were but one vast city—of Earth so populated. The authors did not know when they wrote such stories that the problem of feeding such a worldwide city would be insoluble. That humanity could not stand it, and would not want to stand it. They did not know of the experiments with psychology wherein rats and other laboratory animals were tested for their ability to get along in crowded quarters. There was a limit, after which the beasts turned on each other, became neurotic, touchy, short-tempered.

Just like people cramped together in ghettos.

Just like people everywhere will be when the world's present population doubles.

In about twenty years' time.

I think of two books that have dealt with conditions of the overpopulated Earth. Harry Harrison's novel *Make Room! Make Room!* published in 1966 was the first of these. The time is 1999. The scene is Manhattan Island, in New York City. Harrison says that the population of the city then will be 35 million. It's not at all improbable.

I live in New York and work on Manhattan. It's getting pretty intolerable now, and I doubt that the population is over 10 million (in the middle of the workday). The streets are visibly more crowded, the subways and buses definitely so, more than in years past, and to drive a car through Manhattan at midday is a feat of patience and snaillike progress. Ask anyone about apartment hunting there now. Then consider the city in 1999.

In Harrison's novel his hero is lucky—he shares his one-room apartment with only one other person.

Only a certain number can live comfortably on even the most fertile and fortunate land. The limit is being reached, and that can be demonstrated scientifically.

Isaac Asimov has dealt with this a couple of times in his science articles in the science-fiction magazines. In the May, 1969, issue of *Fantasy and Science Fiction* magazine Asimov, without getting too panicky, reads the doom of humanity in quite simple but unmistakable words. I will quote him, he does it so well:

> I live, immersed in my work and in my content, in the richest nation on Earth, in the period of that nation's maximum power. What a pity, then, that it is all illusion and that I cannot blind myself to the truth. My island of comfort is but a quiet bubble in a torrent that is heaving its way downhill to utter catastrophe. I see nothing to stand in its way and can only watch in helpless horror. The matter can be expressed in a single word: Population.

He then proceeds to demonstrate just how many people the world can support, just how much is needed in air and food and sunlight to feed the maximum number of inhabitants, and just how the rate of population rise grows and has grown. The outlook is pretty grim; pretty nearly unanswerable.

John Brunner tackled the problem head on in his 1968 blockbuster of a novel *Stand on Zanzibar*. The title is ominous in itself. It is based on a belief that about the time of World War I you could stand the entire human race on the 147-square-mile Isle of Wight, elbow to elbow and face to face. In the 1960's the figuring went that it would take the 221 square miles of the Isle of Man to pack us all in like sardines. By 2100, says John Brunner, you'd need the 640 square miles of Zanzibar to do it.

He didn't say where we'd have to be sardined by 2300—probably on the entire continental surface of Earth. But he didn't have to. Zanzibar will be enough—by then we will be in a snarling rage at each other, already at the breaking point.

By then, says Brunner, the year 2010, the streets of any city will be such jungles that you will take your life in your hands to walk in them. The nations will exist on the barest of terms with each other and various states of undeclared war will be perpetual. Sabotage, riot, treachery, and assassination will be the standard accepted activities of a steadily growing mass of the ordinary people.

Do not let me give you the idea that *Stand on Zanzibar* is a simple book. It is a highly complex book, a vast compendium of conjecture and thought, of possibilities and potentials, with several plots and subplots. Brunner is, as you may surmise by his reference to islands like Wight and Man, English. Nevertheless, he did an amazing job of projecting a future America. He has used his eyes and his ears wisely and discerningly.

The book is not entertaining reading—what book could be with such a theme? Harrison's book is scarcely escape reading either. In some ways Brunner overdid it, crowded in too many innovations, too many themes, even as his world was overcrowded. To make matters worse—or perhaps to assist in bringing up a wealth of new ideas—he adopted the style of John Dos Passos' classic novel *U.S.A.* It makes for disconnected reading.

The book carried off the Hugo award that science-fiction readers give every year to the best of the genre. It will be some time before another work as massive and as packed comes along. Yet it was not Brunner's only such massive job dealing with an overpacked future. In 1969 Ace Books published his *The Jagged Orbit*, another blockbuster of a novel, this time taking place in 2014, and with very much the same style. This one concentrates on racial antagonisms in the rat-trap conditions of an overpopulated America. You get a pretty vivid idea of what it will take for an agile man to get along by then—sidearms, protective clothing, respirator, helmet, first-aid kit, and assorted subsidiary weapons. That's for going down to the corner store. If you have to. Better not try.

All very sour. All very grim. All quite unanswerable. If the population continues to grow, that is how it is going to be. Science-fiction writers take note. That is a hurdle that must be overcome by mankind if we are to get on with exploring the rest of this solar system and go on to the system of star colonies and all that is promised thereafter. Mankind may have immortality in the stars, as a species, but only if we can get past the rest of this century.

I do not object to publishing stories of the far future. They represent flags of hope. We do have a future worth living and fighting and working for. But we have immediate objectives that must be overcome in this, our own lifetime, our own century already in its final third. Pollution, overpopulation, the Bomb.

Overpopulation is at least a little coming to the public consciousness. Nothing very much is being done about it so far. Some talk of the Pill, of easier abortion laws, nothing much really. It had better be acted on soon, or else . . . make room! make room! Elbow to elbow, and face to face.

13

Growing Up Grim

THERE IS ONE rather obvious solution to the overpopulation problem. That is to kill off a large section of the world's population by war. A really large section—no piddling stuff like a few tens of thousands in Korea, or a few hundreds of thousands in Vietnam, or a few dozen millions in World War II. Unrestricted germ warfare might do it. Excuse me, that word "unrestricted" is redundant. There is no restriction possible on germ warfare. Germs have no nationality, no patriotism. They are all absolute egalitarians. They are color blind. Sent to kill men in green or black or gray, they will turn around and go to work on khaki and blue with complete lack of bias. And their wives. And their children. And maybe their cattle and sheep and chickens.

Under conditions of elbow-to-elbow living, the tempers of military men and government leaders may prove a lot less approachable to reason than those of today's leaders. Germ warfare is supposed to be outlawed, and the stockpiles of germs and gases eliminated. But politicians' promises tend to be submerged by future events and generals' ambitions.

We have had stories of the world devastated by plague. We have had them for a long time. They go right back to the oldest days. Verne had a story, *The Eternal Adam,* in which cataclysms destroy the human race, save for a handful. This was his very last novella; he is said to have dictated it from his deathbed. His disaster is never explained—possibly he meant to but there was scarce time to rewrite under such circumstances! (It is included in his book *Yesterday and Tomorrow.*)

The best of such novels may be George R. Stewart's *Earth Abides.* A 1949 novel of great power and skill, it was one of the first to be awarded a prize by science-fiction fandom officially. It is not a novel of warfare—a lethal disease, possibly mutated by an act of nature, wipes out all but a few fortunately immune survivors. *Earth Abides* deals then with their efforts to come to terms with an empty world, to settle their problems on a near-deserted land where cities and factories and homes still stand—with none to utilize them.

But it was not an act of war. It could have been caused by radiation. Concern about the effects of radiation on germs and plants and living beings was strong back in 1948 and 1949. Soon several other bombs had gone off. The radiation level of the entire world rose at that time. The world has never been the same since. We are all, everything living and nonliving, more radioactive now than we all were in 1944 and for all the millions of years before that.

There is something different in the postwar world. Atomic power misused to make a bomb. Atomic power misused for war weapons. The threat of atomic fusion used to destroy the enemy in time of war. The enemy—meaning all of us. It takes two sides to make a war. When both sides have the Bomb, both sides contain enemies.

Which we all know perfectly well, and have known since

1945. An entire generation has grown up in this knowledge. It does make a difference. When my generation was growing up we knew that we might have wars to fight and depressions to live through. The world might fall again into the hands of tyrannies, as it had in centuries past. But mankind would survive. Hitler might be frightening to contemplate, but mankind could survive even under a Hitler world. Five hundred years would blunt any tyranny. It always had.

We have a generation now that has grown up to believe that it cannot and will not survive a war fought with atomic weapons. The fallout alone, the half-life of radioactivated land and air . . . Bad scene.

This is also a generation that has grown up in the science-fiction world of today. It was weaned on the atomic war scene. There have been lots of stories and lots of novels about the world after the atomic war. There have been lots of stories too about the atomic war itself—the moment of truth, as it were, when the human bull sees the sword poised and flashing toward him.

I was thinking the other day of Ace Books' most unsuspected best seller, a novel I reprinted in 1954, and whose title I changed to *Daybreak, 2250 A.D.* It was written by Andre Norton as a juvenile novel, and it was her first science-fiction book-length work. She called it *Star Man's Son,* and it was published in 1952 by Harcourt, Brace and Company. I believe their edition is still in print and still sold as a children's book.

The Ace edition's cover shows a white-haired boy in fur loincloth and primitive gear poling a raft across a river which is spanned by a shattered but clearly twentieth-century bridge. It has sold continuously and rapidly for fifteen years, in printing after printing, with steady price rises to meet the rising costs of production, has broken the record for any book ever published by what has become a major paperback publisher, and continues to sell with unabated interest. Well over a million copies would be my conservative estimate of its total sale to date.

There is nothing in our Ace edition to indicate that it is supposed to be a juvenile novel. You can assume it from the fact that its hero, Fors of the Puma Clan, is a teen-ager who has not yet been accepted into full manhood in his primitive tribe living high up in the mountains. The story tells of how Fors gains his "Star" rating—the tribal equivalent of warriorhood—by going on a daring expedition into the taboo mystery lands of the level plains.

Andre Norton wrote the book for children—twelve and up, says the flyleaf on the original edition. And I am quite sure that it has been youth, twelve and up, that has made up the bulk of its readers over these many years. And what is it that these children have been, as it were, weaned on?

Fors of the Puma Clan, we are told from the start, has been in trouble with his tribe because he has white hair, which marks him as that dreaded of all things, a mutant.

> Mutant! For more than two hundred years—ever since the black days of chaos following the Great Blow-up, the atomic-war—that cry had been enough to condemn without trial. . . . Ugly tales were told of what had happened to the mutants, those unfortunates born in the first year after the Blow-up. Some tribes had taken drastic steps in those days to see that the strain of human—or almost human—lineage be kept pure. Here in the Eyrie, far apart from the infection of the bombed sectors, mutation had been almost unknown. But he, Fors, had Plains' blood—tainted, unclean—and, since he could remember at all, he had never been allowed to put that fact from him.

What these children have been weaned on is the matter-of-fact presumption that an atomic war will destroy the United States and every other known nation, will reduce the world to primitive conditions again, render most of its surface uninhabitable, deadly, dangerous, and alter the shape and form of what life may survive.

They read, without blinking an eyelash, an adventure of a character similar to a primitive Indian, full of superstition and backwoods ignorance, who pursues his dangerous expedition across a world filled with the ruins of a once-mighty but now incomprehensible civilization. They see that world now the habitat of beasts such as never existed in our time, of monsters gifted with intelligence beyond that of animals, and of men cursed with radiation changes that have made them literally a nonhuman race.

The children take this information in their stride—it is, after

all, not new to them. They have heard of the Bomb before reaching the reading stage of such novels. They have heard of what
might happen. They know about mutations and what they could
mean. They take it all for granted. And in *Daybreak, 2250 A.D.*
they enjoy an adventure story laid in what is obviously a believable, and, God help us, even predictably probable future.

The point I am making is that the people who read this book
must number millions—one can assume that every hard-cover
book sold is probably read by a dozen or so young people, and
every paperback edition possibly gains a handful of readers too,
especially if the purchaser is young. Five million, ten million,
can that be the number who have read Andre Norton's post-
atomic war novel? And that was over fifteen years. A lot of them
—most of them—have grown up now. People who read this—and
novels of a similar premise, for there were many around with
the same sort of postatomic war backgrounds—must now be in
their twenties and even thirties. They must be engineers, doctors,
businessmen, technicians, soldiers, even fathers and mothers,
housewives and schoolteachers. And to be sure a large segment
must still be in college or doing their stint in the armed forces.

They all take it for granted that an atomic war will spell the
end of mankind and civilization as we know it. They have taken
if for granted since their childhood. They do not question that
fact.

It must have influenced their thinking. It must influence what
they do and say now.

It is a science-fiction concept that has been absorbed into the
modern scene.

14

To Be or Not to Be

I WAS BORN in 1914, the year that might be said to have really
been the close of the nineteenth century in a cultural and political sense. I grew up in a changed world, but not a world where

the knowledge of doom was an accepted fact. It is hard for my generation to realize what it must be to have grown up in the generation that took and takes *Daybreak, 2250 A.D.*, for granted, as just a good science-fiction adventure of the future, no questions asked.

When I see and read about modern youth, about their rebellion against accepted standards, about their espousal of such escape mechanisms as pot and dope and weird philosophies, their efforts at establishing instant Utopian colonies, and their rejection of the standards of the generations that preceded them, I am not surprised. What else did anyone expect of the generation that grew up knowing the Atom Bomb was waiting in the wings?

We who dreamed of atomic power back in the thirties thought it would lead to Utopia. We saw atomic energy lighting the cities and powering the factories for free, powering our flights to the planets, pushing luxurious vast airplanes through the skies, leading to plenty for all.

The youth of today knew better. They were raised to know that they faced the caves again—if they survived, that is. They knew that atomic power plants are built first to power giant submarines laden with atomic rockets to help destroy the world. Atomic power plants for peaceful use—they are a superfluous expense, a rarity.

They also have had ideals instilled by science fiction, not by other sources. This generation believes in science fiction, it runs like a thread through its "underground" newspapers and through its works. The young people have read novels about atomic aftermath. They have also read such stories as *Thunder and Roses* by Theodore Sturgeon. It helped give them something of a political ideal all their own, something for their generation only.

Thunder and Roses is a short story, first published in 1955, reprinted in *A Way Home*, which is a collection of Sturgeon's stories. It is a simple story, told with the skill of a master. Emotional, deep, sensitive, written at the peak of Sturgeon's powers and the greatest intensity of his feeling. It is the story of a couple of young men in control of a secret atomic rocket launching post. It is the story of their thoughts, their hearts, their emotions when they learn that an enemy attack has destroyed America, that their loved ones are probably dead, that they alone have the means of retribution in their hands. Their defense post has survived, unknown to the foe.

Shall they launch their atomic rockets and do to the enemy what he has already done to their homeland? That is the problem. Retribution . . . is it right, or would their firing also signify the end of all humanity? The air was already polluted, perhaps no one in America survived. But over there, on the other side, obviously the enemy was alive. It was in their power to destroy that remaining half of humanity.

In the end, the man who favors retribution at all costs is knocked out by the other. While he is unconscious, the remaining American rips the launching mechanisms to pieces. He then goes outside into the polluted atmosphere, sits down. The story ends this way:

> "You'll have your chance," he said into the far future. "And by heaven, you'd better make good."

After that he just waited.

That is another way science fiction answered the problem of the atomic bomb. It is presumably a lesson that must have sunk deep into the mind, possibly the unconscious mind, of hundreds of thousands who have read that story—the same ones who read Andre Norton and the others.

In many readers it instilled one belief—that humanity may survive the atomic war after all. And if we survive, no matter how few, we can reconstruct civilization and fulfill the destiny that awaits us in the stars.

You can find this theme tucked into the background of some Galactic Empire novels—that Terra is a half-devastated world whose sons had to take to the stars to find better worlds. The progression to Galactic Empire and beyond is not halted by a brief hiatus in Terrestrial civilization. What is a few thousand years' delay in the historical canvas of infinity?

But are there no stories in which the atomic war never occurs? To be sure, but they are not too convincing. Not with overpopulation and the attendant madness advancing so rapidly.

Nature has a way of paring down animal populations when

they get beyond their normal food-death cycles. Wolves starve when they wipe out too many rabbits. Deer starve when they overextend their numbers without having been hunted. Lemmings dash madly into the sea when they have become too numerous for sustenance. Maladies have been charted which periodically cut back the numbers of certain species.

In the past, plagues and famines and droughts have consistently cut back the human ranks. But we have outsmarted all that. We know too much now, and our numbers are growing beyond nature's capacity. But nature may have a trick or two left. Madness of numbers, fury at close quarters, the dropping away of natural vitamins and natural sun-originated food elements may affect our capacities to resist mutant diseases and our capacity to reason logically. We do have the atomic bomb in storage in many nations. Despite the best resolve never to use it—miraculously it has not yet been used in twenty-five years of revolutions and wars—pressures build up as populations build up. It may prove to be nature's way after all.

In his article about population, which I have quoted once, Asimov does not predict the use of the atomic bomb. He makes no specific predictions. He does say:

> If we do nothing but what comes naturally, the population increase will be brought to a halt by an inevitable rise in the death rate through the wars and civil rioting that worsening human friction and desperation will bring. . . . There is a race in man's future between a death-rate rise and a birth-rate decline, and by 2000, if the latter doesn't win, the former will.

Mankind may get some sense in time. As a science-fictionist I have faith. I must admit that I have not seen any s-f novels that pointed to a believable way out. S-f novels and writers persist in pointing toward the obvious, that Sunset, 2000 A.D. which will not see the sun rise again until 2250 or later.

Andre Norton was not the only one, as I said. Others predicted it back when it counted. Leigh Brackett's *The Long Tomorrow* —she thought that the Dark Ages to come might be sustained by isolated farm communities like the Amish. Poul Anderson has written several novels of the post-atomic bomb world, including

Twilight World and *After Doomsday*. Many others, many theories, many viewpoints, many scenes. *On the Beach* by Nevil Shute is the supreme pessimistic view—not surprising since the author is not among the ranks of deep-dyed s-f writers. We s-f writers rarely let the world die. We have the farther vision. It sustains us.

15

Misreading the Maps

AFTER THAT, if you are still hanging on, it seems reasonable to turn to a book published ten years ago with the ominous title of *New Maps of Hell*. The writer was an English literary scholar named Kingsley Amis and the book purported to be a study of science fiction as he found it at that time. Considering what we have been talking about, one would suppose that the mapping of hells would have dealt with something of the same deadly serious subjects we have just discussed.

But you would be wrong. Mr. Amis' maps of hell are what he considers science fiction to be—a sort of suet pudding of literary trash with here and there a nice plum of vicious social satire sticking out and worth examining. He seems to have a special fondness for Utopias that are not Utopias, for instance.

I should not do Mr. Amis wrong: he declares himself a science-fiction addict at the very start, though he then is careful not to identify himself more closely with it than that. As a matter of fact Mr. Amis is a mainstream writer who occasionally likes to read some science fiction, and had the good fortune to talk someone into allowing him to do a witty little book about it.

I get the distinct impression that, while investigating his subject, he was being given a guided and selected tour through one particular publisher's s-f mill, for he seems to be most familiar with the works of its authors and most especially with the writings of Frederik Pohl, whom he calls the "most consistently able writer science fiction, in the modern sense, has yet produced." He devotes a good deal of space to a rather admiring analysis of several of Frederik Pohl's satirical works—quite clearly he digs the scene of Pohl's satire on advertising, *The Space Merchants,* for he quotes with evident familiarity scenes and dialogues, none of which could by any standard be calculated to spark that sense of wonder which is the mainspring of the devotee.

Now, I cannot deny that Frederik Pohl is indeed one of the cleverest minds in the field. His short stories and novelettes are gems of cunning, unusual ideas, delectable twists of the satirical dagger here and there, and decidedly entertaining. I have known Fred myself since our fandom days—we were both active Futurians when that was one of the noisier fan clubs of the thirties—a germinal club whose members have since become prime movers of the science-fiction world that colors society today. He showed early a capacity for plot construction, for clever turns of a phrase, for strikingly novel ideas. He was more than usually egotistical as well—but since when is that a crime for a creative mind?

It is clear that the talents he displayed then he matured later. Kingsley Amis and Frederik Pohl obviously struck a responsive chord in each other—Amis too has a deft hand at social satire and it is not therefore so remarkable that for him Pohl was tops.

Pohl is, like most of us who came out of the Depression, something of a disillusioned idealist, a latter-day cynic. I think, however, that, while I have continued to retain my faith in humanity and in the future, Pohl long ago scrapped his. His satires are sincere.

I must admit that, while I usually find Pohl's short stories and novelettes fascinating, there is something about his novels which gives me the fidgets. They are indeed the new maps of hell which Mr. Amis admired enough to give his entire study of science fiction that title.

The trouble with this arch kind of study of our field is that the critic simply has not been steeped in it long enough. He does not reach the dyed-in-the-wool reader. He cannot reach the man who once read s-f exhaustively for four or five formative years before going on to create some version of the future in a laboratory—those engineers, technicians, experimenters of today who have passed their grounding in s-f ideation and are now trying to build the future.

I started out by saying this is a science-fiction world and that the writings of the field have clearly shaped this world of today —for better or for worse. But Mr. Amis does not know it. For him I. Asimov is a man who wrote a story about robots. Olaf Stapledon is not mentioned. He cannot distinguish between Wellsian and Vernian. And I don't think he ever heard of the Galactic Empire and its Decline and Fall.

He has a good time with some of the trivia around—a few of the short stories of the day—some of the lesser works that make up the bulk of any particular year's output. He dismisses Van Vogt as a creator of supermen. And of course he goes into the usual song and dance about how too few s-f writers pay attention to character development and how too many stress only ideas and gimmicks. If they would pay more attention to turning out really fine character novels, why, then, the mainstream would stop labeling them as a low category not to be reviewed and might start accepting them as mainstream writers.

It is ten years later. I have already indicated that the lists of best sellers do contain works that must be defined as science fiction. They had to come to our field to do it. Alas, we have still no one to post against such great mainstream novels as *Portnoy's Complaint, The Love Machine, The Arrangement,* and the rest of that constant stream of psychiatrists' couch and bedroom agonies that mark the triumphs of the mainstream.

No, Mr. Amis, science fiction does not consist of new maps of hell. It does consist of endless charts of the paths open to triumphant mankind. Social satire, the bitter skewering of some of the odious aspects of the present, are but a part of our category. They are parts, not the whole. They are but one of the many facets of our infinite explorations into the unknown side of existence.

There is a persistent pattern of wailing to be found among certain critics and some writers demanding that science fiction be accepted as part of the mainstream of literature. They dislike having their novels labeled as part of a category, like mysteries and westerns. Their work, they declare, is as good as many novels by nonfantasy writers and ought to be treated by book reviewers and bookstores in similar fashion. This business of labeling gives them the horrors; they feel that it diminishes them.

I have never agreed with this. Our audience is not that of the mainstream. Our influence is specialized and what we do has a different effect than the general run of mainstream fiction, from best sellers to the remaindered losers. We are, in fact, as specialized a form as the mystery novel, so why the fuss?

But the fuss will continue. Only recently at the annual awards banquet of the Science Fiction Writers of America, a newly ordained editor for a book firm made a speech reiterating the old cry. He said, in part: "Labeling a book as s-f puts a stigma on it. Many reviewers won't even bother to look at a book if its jacket screams that it's fantasy. . . . S-f writers should assert themselves and let their books compete with the mainstream of the publishing output not as 'science fiction novels' but simply as 'novels.' "

So he published a whole series of s-f books in very nearly uniform format which did not say s-f on their covers and whose cover drawings were fairly ambiguous. Did he succeed in fooling the reviewers? Not so you could tell. Anyone intelligent enough to pay out money for hard-cover books knew what he was buying. If he didn't like s-f, he didn't buy.

As a matter of fact, labeling books "s-f" is the established technique these days of publishers who really do know their business. It is done all the time in Great Britain by such successful publishers as Gollancz, Sidgwick and Jackson, Dennis Dobson, Macdonald—their books are clearly identified with the words or their abbreviations. So, too, Doubleday and others in the United States—and consistently by almost all the paperback houses here.

Science-fiction readers do not want mainstream fiction. It is mainstream readers who occasionally must come to us for a best seller. That is when the label is missing.

But by and large mainstream fiction is literature that deals with the here and now, with people and events as they are, and which does not require the addition of the kinds of fantasy I enumerated. It is to mainstream writers we look if we want to find talented depiction of modern man in his travails. It is to science fiction we turn only if we want to get away from the travails of today to gain the broader vision of what might be, what might have been, what is yet to come.

Why should so many s-f writers therefore continue to hunger for the glory of being submerged in the world of general un-categorized fiction? There are several probable answers. They value the reviews and praise of critics whose comments grace the daily newspapers—people like Kingsley Amis. They want the bookstores to display their books in the windows for the sake of glory. They would like the Literary Guild and the Book-of-the-Month Club to tap their books and make them famous and rich and all that.

All very normal desires. All very admirable. Overlooking the various economic and publishing politics that determine what gets reviewed and what does not, and what gets book-clubbed and what does not, the best way to attain these objectives would be to give up writing what you want to write—science fiction—and write what you think the little group of "name" reviewers will praise. The fact that these writers do not take this course is evidence either that they are incapable of it or else that they really are as hooked on s-f as all of us and wouldn't be at home outside the field. I think the latter is the reality.

Since contradiction and what dialecticians call the interpene-tration of opposites are the essence of controversial thinking, I shall now do an about-face and discuss a writer who has always considered himself of the mainstream, rejects the claim to being a science-fiction writer, whose works are reviewed with respect and enthusiasm by the literary pundits of America, and who, by God, deserves every word of it and is, in my opinion, one of the most originally brilliant science-fiction writers going. I refer to Kurt Vonnegut, Jr.

16

Delivering a Cosmic Telegram

I'VE ALREADY TALKED about Vonnegut when I was discussing his *Slaughterhouse Five* at the start of this book. Of Vonnegut's seven hard-cover books, four are distinctly in the science-fiction genre and the other three are spectacular in their own way. What makes him, then, a mainstream writer rather than a science-fiction writer?

The answer is because he says so, because he never wrote for the pulps or the category magazines and because he gets the highest rates for his writings—much higher than the sums paid by the standard s-f publishers. What strange luck is it that enabled him to avoid what some of the would-be mainstream s-f writers regard as their pitfalls? Who can say? I only know that Vonnegut is unique, that he apparently caters to nobody in his storytelling, that he has a positively scintillating cynicism the like of which cannot be found elsewhere, that he packs his books with razor-edged social comments, that he apparently does not seem to take his science-fiction elements with that often deadly seriousness that so many of our regulars do.

It isn't easy. That is probably the secret. His novels have a subtle complexity that do not follow routine and his ideas are often so startlingly different as at first to seem purely whacky— except that they are not. There's no real arguing with them. Whacky as they might seem, they have a logic inherent to themselves which is often not of this world.

If this confuses you, you'll have to read Vonnegut yourself. A universe maker he most certainly is and he builds on a tangent that no one else either sees or had the infernal brass to tackle.

Let's take *The Sirens of Titan*. This one, whose title sounds like a Burroughs epic, was first published in a paperback edition. It made an historic breakthrough in the relationship between paperbacks and hard-covers. For I recall it as the first paper-back original to go from the cheap to the expensive edition, rather than vice versa. It was reprinted in hard covers—presumably by public demand. Lately this course has been followed by other paperbacks, but it took Vonnegut to reverse the field. Which is characteristic.

Consider *The Sirens of Titan* then. I'll not summarize, because I can't in this space. One theme, one of many, is very galactic. A starship is en route from one end of the cosmos to the other. Its mission is simply to bear greetings from one superintelligent species to another. No interchange of art or commerce or such—just greetings. The starship needs repairs. It pauses at an obscure sun and planets system in an obscure and unimportant section of an unimportant galaxy. It requires a few manufactured parts to replace some broken bits of the engine. The planetary system contains no intelligent life. One planet of the group, however, is fertile and swarming with lower orders.

The space travelers therefore have the means of obtaining their replacement parts. They intervene in this world very briefly in order to start one of the species on that planet to evolving upward. Then they sit back on the Saturnian moon known as Titan, and simply wait for the inevitable. They have plenty of time; they are quite prepared to wait a hundred million years. They do.

The species evolves, it works its way up to primitive tool-using levels, works its way up to making fire, learns how to utilize metals, develops civilization, finally reaches its technological period where it has factories and engineers and tool designers, and so on. When it has reached this point, our starship's engineer goes back to the planet, places an order for the missing parts, gets them, returns to his starship, makes the repairs, and takes off to resume his cosmic telegram delivery!

The planet is Earth. The species is man. And we have been calmly told by author Vonnegut that the sole purpose of all human history and evolution is to fulfill that one mission—deliver the engine parts—after which humanity can sink back into oblivion for all the sponsors of our evolution are concerned. The scale on which they live and think is totally out of our league.

This is but one of the themes in the novel. There are lots more. Vonnegut's *Cat's Cradle* is possibly the equal of the *Sirens* in astonishing novelties. We get something of what may or may not be Vonnegut's philosophy in the religion called Bokononism introduced as part of the many elements of this cat's cradle of a novel. If the sayings of Bokonon have not gained the popularity accorded to Heinlein's water-sharing cult of *Stranger in a Strange Land* it is probably only because Bokonon is infinitely more cynical and yet far simpler. Youth is not yet that devoid of faith.

There is a quote from the First Book of Bokonon which is perhaps relevant to the purpose of mankind as given in *The Sirens of Titan*. Let me cite it:

> . . . God created every living creature that now moveth, and one was man. Mud as man alone could speak. God leaned close as mud as man sat up, looked around, and spoke. Man blinked. "What is the purpose of all this?" he asked politely.
> "Everything must have a purpose?" asked God.
> "Certainly," said man.
> "Then I leave it to you to think of one for all this," said God. And He went away.

This is, in a manner of speaking, Vonnegut's cosmic viewpoint. If existence has a purpose, he hasn't been able to determine it.

Vonnegut, who occasionally does not hesitate to intrude himself in his own novels, will sometimes repeat a character in two or more of his books. He has a science-fiction novelist named Kilgore Trout pop up in *God Bless You, Mr. Rosewater* (which is otherwise not one of his s-f books) and also in *Slaughterhouse Five*. Kilgore Trout has written some eighty-seven science-fiction space opera—and still has to hold a menial job in order to keep from starving to death. That may be a hint as to why Vonnegut prefers not to think of himself as being in the category. It is a bit rough, and things are really not at all that bad for professional s-f writers. But as Vonnegut himself would say, so it goes.

Similarly the American Nazi who shows up to lecture the American POWs in *Slaughterhouse Five* is the principal character of the novel *Mother Night*. A most complex character who may or may not be what he seems to be, this tall American is a man of easy speaking ability and considerable literary talent, a man of vigorous ingenuity, lots of originality, and spectacular frustrations. His name is Howard W. Campbell, Jr.

17

A Victorious Vernian

JOHN W. CAMPBELL, JR., is the editor and moving force behind the largest-selling s-f magazine, *Analog*. When Campbell, at that time one of the best writers of space opera of the thirties—his novels rivaled those of Edward E. Smith in style and popularity —became editor of *Astounding Stories* in 1937 it was an event which is generally credited as being the start of the change in the genre from the rather obvious pulp that had gone before to a far more sophisticated style of writing, more serious and complex plotting, and a generally more mature approach. Campbell's editing direction has always been hailed as the basis for this step upward in the whole field.

Let us examine this a bit more closely.

The one thing Campbell did do was to work a change of title away from the rather awful appellation "Astounding," which was an imitation of the original magazine title "Amazing" and in the worst tradition of the most garish days of the pulps. Campbell did not get his change through completely for some time, but he did get the title changed to *Astounding Science Fiction*, tried a few variations in relative sizes of the logo and eventually managed to signal a real maturation of the magazine with the title of *Analog*.

However, the question of whether it was Campbell personally who selected, chose, directed, and made authors revise until the field was upgraded is one of those "iffy" things which can never be resolved. For it seems to me that what happened is that the golden days of the forties, which are credited to Campbell's magazine, the days when a flood of really good writers began to show up with style and skill and ingenuity, represented something a little different. They were actually the first generation of writers who had grown up on science fiction, had been grounded and, as it were, schooled in science fiction and hence were able to utilize this in advancing further. Science fiction builds upon science fiction—and in the fact that magazines had been publishing s-f under that label since 1926 lay the reason why this generation of writers reached their twenties in time to write for Campbell when he, who was also a first-generation writer raised in the same school, was waiting and looking for better stuff. Campbell became an editor when the field itself came of age. Because he himself had mastered the field as it stood and because he himself, as an author, had fought to build upon what had been, he was able to recognize and assist those of his own generation.

Before that, in the late twenties and through the thirties, the men who wrote for the three or four science-fiction pulps—*Amazing, Wonder, Astounding*—had had their grounding in the general pulps. Their source of original foundations had been such magazines as *Argosy, Blue Book,* or worse. Such newcomers to s-f as began to show up in the pulps were very young —high school students, college freshmen—I sold my first story to *Wonder Stories* when I was eighteen. Very few of us had any kind of real grounding in science. Campbell himself sold a group of interstellar novels before he had his college diploma. And he went into editing directly afterward.

So what he found was the first fresh flood of developed science-fiction thinkers, men like Heinlein, Simak, and Asimov who had not been tarred with the old pulp styles and who were already sufficiently advanced in modern scientific study as to be aware that mechanistic universes à la Ray Cummings, George Allen England, and Homer Eon Flint were already passé.

However, let us not deny that Campbell was the right person in the right place to give these writers recognition and to direct them in advancing further. There were pulp magazines aplenty in those days—the paperbacks had not yet begun to wash them away, as they did after the war was over. These pulps were edited by a breed of men who had learned what publishers of pulps expected of their editors—breathless titles, lurid covers, fast-action plots, and short easy-to-read paragraphs. John Campbell became a pulp editor too, but with one magazine to produce a month (as against the four, six, or eight that some of his colleagues had to contend with) he had the time to do a better job than usual, to give more attention to each story, to avoid the mistakes that the pulp-trained editors of *Wonder* and *Startling* and *Planet Stories* and *Amazing* were making. Campbell had the time and the understanding that they did not have.

I think, however, that the enigma of John W. Campbell today is partly answered by the role he now occupies in the paleontology of publishing. He is a living fossil; he is just about the last pulp editor still in business, still working on the same single title as when he started. He may hold the world's record for the longest continuous run on a single pulp magazine—1937 to date— well over thirty years. Though *Analog* is not printed on pulp paper, has a fine typographical setup (the best of any of the s-f periodicals), it is still technically the same genus of story magazine that all pulps were. It must be a frustrating thing for one man, so talented, to find himself in such a perpetual and isolated role. It is to that frustration that I place my own guess as to what makes Campbell tick.

To begin with, Campbell was aware, more so than most, of the dynamic era of science that was opening up after the war. He was aware of the potentials of science-fiction thinking for the working scientist when funds for research started to become virtually unlimited during the war and even more so afterward. He himself was a mine of new concepts—concepts which he gave freely to his writers and which sparkled and bounced through the pages of his magazine—he surely must have been charged with the need to join in that research, to partake of the wonders being discovered, to contribute his share and have his share of glory. But this was not to be. He was stuck where he was. He tried at one time to launch a general science magazine, even managed to get control of one for two or three numbers, but it proved a washout. So it was *Astounding* which had to be his workshop, his laboratory, his platform for glory.

You can't do much with a magazine outside of editorializing, and he began to do that. Then he made his first world-shaking offering—he "discovered" a scientific system which would shake the world and produce a new breed of supermen. Dianetics burst forth into the world's view in the pages of John W. Campbell, Jr.'s, *Astounding*.

Dianetics went its way, made a brief stir in America, gathered an assortment of honest but naïve experimenters and gullible guinea pigs and then quietly exited from the pages of Campbell's magazine. It represented one of Campbell's great blind spots—a mechanistic approach to psychology, sociology, and history. Campbell, grounded in physics and chemistry, has always approached humanity and the humanities with the supposition that the human mind and the human psyche can be handled in a laboratory with the techniques and impersonal methodology of the exact sciences. (Curiously, exactly the same approach that Karl Marx and Friedrich Engels attempted to use a century earlier, though they were in rebellion against the social order whereas Campbell seems to regard the social order of his time as the True Mathematical Fact not to be questioned any more than one would quarrel with an axiom of simple arithmetic.)

Dianetics went underground, emerged as the Church of Scientology, and may yet become the Neo-Mormonism of the twentieth century. Campbell may indeed have influenced his time more than he would like to know. Scientology is a movement of dangerous dimensions, great wealth, and sufficiently subversive mind-warping techniques to get it banned in many parts of the civilized world.

But Campbell seems to have realized that he had goofed with dianetics. He lay low for a while, then began playing around with a new series of discoveries. He discovered all by himself what the occultists and the psychic researchers had been dabbling with for a century. He discovered what he called "psi" powers, and for a number of years his magazine—and consequently the rest of the s-f literary world (for the highest paying market can set the tune and the overflow must run into the lower paying markets)—read like an educated and literary version of the bulletin of the Society for Psychic Research. Dowsing, telekinesis, telepathy, clairvoyance, pyromancy, and all the rest of

the paraphernalia of the Victorian séances and mediums were
paraded out in new forms, labeled "mutant" powers, and his
readers were urged to look with an open mind upon these
marvels of the psychic.

They did that. Because by then his readers were primarily
men working in the engineering sciences, men who were as
poorly grounded in psychology, history, theology, and sociology
as Campbell himself.

The psi stories petered away too, and John Campbell turned
to the affairs of the world. If he couldn't make a scientific discovery that would bear his mark, he'd at least advance his own
original thinking about the affairs of humanity. Politics and
social organization would be his oyster. What emerged from this
was a series of glib, logical-sounding, very scientifically worded,
and able literary lectures to his readers about how there really
are superior and inferior people, about the idiocy of tampering
with the profit motive, of the value of greed as a driving mechanism, of the inevitability and desirability of war as a natural
outlet for a naturally aggressive race, of the superiority of the
United States over all other countries and forms of government,
well—the gamut.

Jules Verne was fascinated by the gimmicks and coming inventions of science, but he never quarreled with his class or his
government. He was a French patriot, a French imperialist, a
loyal supporter of his flag and country. No internationalist he.

John W. Campbell, Jr., a century later is also fascinated by
the gimmicks and technological inventions of science, and he
too is a patriot, an imperialist, a loyal supporter of his flag and
country. No internationalist he.

Analog with Campbell represents the Vernian faction in
science fiction today.

Yet Campbell is not in any way a fool. He is doing exactly the
right thing for the readers of his magazine. He knows who they
are, he caters to them, and they approve and support his magazine. For men who are making their living in scientific research
today must be, in the majority, men working for corporations
and industries operating on defense contracts. That's where the
money is in research. To hold a job in such a laboratory you

must have a security clearance. You must pass a series of intense investigations by any or all of several government and military agencies that must prove beyond a doubt that you have never entertained a single subversive thought in your life nor aided or abetted a single improper unpatriotic group or movement. If you want to make a living in research—chemistry, physics, astronautics, aviation, oceanography, etc.—you must be the kind of person who brainwashed yourself from your earliest days in high school right on through college, through postgraduate studies, to this very day.

But if you are also attracted by science, you will probably have passed through a phase of fascination for science fiction. You may, like a surprising number of scientific workers, still enjoy reading science fiction. If so, *Analog* is safe for you. Listing *Analog* as one of your regular reading habits will not get you in bad with any security agency. Campbell may or may not consciously know this, but certainly he is in accord with the Establishment. Upholding the idea of slavery as a practical proposition for the care and best utilization of naturally inferior races may be a shocking reversion that might startle even a John Bircher—but it will never get *Analog* a subversive rating. It is perfectly okay to advocate what *Analog* advocates.

So I must submit that John W. Campbell, Jr., is still the right person for the right magazine. *Analog* has a higher circulation than any of its competitors. Its readers must, to a large degree, be exclusive to it. For mighty few are the Hugos and Nebulas won by *Analog* entries. The highest awards of science fiction in literature and popular reader appeal go fairly consistently to novels and short stories from the pages of *Galaxy, Magazine of Fantasy and Science Fiction,* and the publishers of original novels in book form.

18

Wellsians in Crisis

WHEN I START out in this book saying that this is a world that science fiction made I am not taking either a Vernian or a Wellsian stand. If anything, it is a world that the Vernians made —only lately are we waking up to the rapidly approaching deadlines of pollution, overpopulation, and The Bomb to realize that we have too few Wellsians among the world's political leaders. Our gadgets and gimmicks, our televisions and airplanes and space ships, these are the things in which Verne would rejoice. But it will take more than gadget thinking to solve the equation of the next three decades.

I'd like to make it clear again that when I use the term "Wellsian" I do not mean what used to be called Wellsian socialism. I use it only in the sense that it follows the lead of H. G. Wells toward science fiction—that sociology and human relations merging with modern science are necessary ingredients of science fiction. Whereas I see the Vernian as essentially one accepting the status quo of the system in power, I see the Wellsian taking for granted that social relations will change with the application or lack of application of scientific development.

In the present science-fiction world it is mainly Wellsians who are in a crisis. Vernians go on as unthinkingly as before. It is the writers with social conscience who are increasingly disturbed by the three barriers of the twentieth century. Because we are living day by day among those three terrible challenges and because the Wellsians, aware of what they can mean, feel more and more the ineffectuality of protest and are imaginatively more sensitive to the ultimate disasters portending, it is Wellsians who reflect gloom and hysteria in their works.

In truth it *is* hard to see the forest for the trees. We have to fix our mental vision on a future which grows daily less and less visible. Our future—that of space-oriented humanity, of man bursting his planetary bonds and spreading out to infinity—was glimpsed more clearly in the thirties and forties. Now that we have actually reached the moon, moving across the threshold of that future, the three crises confronting the Terrestrial landscape becloud the view and in their darkening shadows the vision is lost to sight save in the mind's eye. All we can visualize on the day-to-day scene about us is the potential catastrophes of the immediate years to come.

The result has had its effect on science fiction. Many who would presumably be heralding glories to come have become ravens of doom. Cries of disaster are heard in their writings. One of the best expositions of this havoc-crying turned up on my desk just as I was working on this part of the book. It is from the editor's introduction to an anthology by Robert Silverberg of gloomy (mind you!) science fiction entitled *Dark Stars*. Let me quote:

> If the writer perhaps believes that human civilization is a cancerous growth that has already consumed most of one planet and is about to spread to the others, he may not create fiction that sings hosannas to the valiant astronauts and cosmonauts. . . . If the writer thinks that man, for all his remarkable achievements, is nevertheless a flawed, turbulent, potentially dangerous character, as much demon as angel, then the writer will be cautious about applauding man's doings. . . .
>
> Once upon a time the bulk of science fiction was written by cheerful Rotarians eager to leap into the lovely future. That was in the 1930's, when the future still looked pretty good (especially in contrast with the present), and in the 1940's, when the defeat of the bestial Axis foe was supposed to open the gateway to Utopia. But a good chunk of that future has already unveiled itself since those days of s-f's innocence, and what has appeared has not been so inspiring. . . . By measuring the fictional "1963" of 1938 against the real 1963, s-f writers have of necessity suffered a darkening of the vision. Hymns to the miracle that is color television become less meaningful when that screen is so often reddened by the blood of those who were our best.

Utopians, in short, have given way to anti-Utopians. The purpose

of Utopias has always been to hold before humanity the possibilities of our better sides. The anti-Utopians represent those
who have come to deny that the better side can ever triumph.
They hold before humanity the prospect of perpetual defeat.

Humanity is an obstinate and complex beast. I have but to re-
mind myself that this aggressive, scheming, imaginative creature
with all its faults has been around on this planet for many
millions of years during which it has survived every known
disaster of nature—famines, droughts, earthquakes, floods, ice
ages, plagues, beasts, and the attacks of other members of its
own species—and has still managed to dream of marvels, to
create and keep new discoveries for the betterment of its descendants, to develop and cherish art, beauty and song, to work
patiently day by dreary day toward the vision of Utopian concepts, each greater and more heavenly, and that this beast is
not going to suddenly stop this millions-of-years ingrained drive
just because of the shadows of the next thirty years. Utopia
construction is part of our scene. Utopia downgrading has always represented the panicking of the fainthearted and the
pretend-visionary. It is part of the marvelous complexity of a
thinking beast that this is so. It is also a fact that the anti-Utopian
image never achieves the power to move masses of men, whereas
the Utopian concept usually can.

This being so, such downbeat visions as science fiction may
choose to present—the world gone to pot—are taken as a warning
rather than as a serious prediction. Watch out for this shoal and
that—if we want to arrive safely at our spatial port.

Robert Silverberg chose to lead off his collection of downbeat
tales with as black a novelette as has ever been written—one of
the last stories of the late C. M. Kornbluth. Kornbluth, best
remembered today as coauthor of *The Space Merchants* and
Gladiator-at-Law with Frederik Pohl, died young and therefore
the body of his work, signed by himself alone and not as a
collaboration, is limited.

I do not think I can write objectively of Cyril Kornbluth and
I will not try. He and I were good friends back in the days of
the Futurian Society of New York, in years just before the war
and the first year after Pearl Harbor too. The Futurians were a

special group of New York fans, most of us would-be writers or writers in embryo, and we included a surprising number of present-day "big names" among our members. But Cyril was special, even for us. A very young man then—in fact, I believe he was still in high school when he first made contact with us— he rapidly built up close friendships with our group. Yet from the start he had that deep streak of black humor, of alienation, which was to come full bloom in his works after the end of the war. It showed in the subtle touches of cruel comment he could make about our rivals in fandom, it showed in occasional black humor in the midst of conversations and social events, it showed from the first in his earliest writings, his short stories and novelettes published under pen names in the science-fiction magazines which came into existence under Fred Pohl, Bob Lowndes, and myself back in those days.

Yet at that time he was not without his faith in the future— his work was not that black—and he was able to write quite funny pieces and even stories with a dream-desire quality suggestive of the endless ideals that have always moved mankind— the title of one, *The Golden Road,* is evidence of this.

Whatever was in Cyril Kornbluth's roots that embittered him was never quite clear to me. Somehow he was always a little apart from home, school, and society. It was to be the stresses of marriage and war that eventually produced the C. M. Kornbluth of maturity and total alienation. It was these same stresses that severed our close association with him (we had even coauthored several stories, even as Frederik Pohl was to do profitably and extensively after the war). What transpired in the life and inner personality of Cyril Kornbluth during the years 1942–1945 will remain matters for speculation. What counts is that the Kornbluth who made his real mark on the world of science fiction was a bitter, acid individual, a hermit by choice, dominated by an alienation with the world as it existed and mankind as it is, and plowing his vindictiveness into his short stories and novelettes. His novels are models of sharp depiction, lucid writing, and they have never had quite the despairing basis that he allowed his shorter work to display. Unfortunately time has not dealt kindly with the three novels he signed, which were presumably done without collaboration. One of them dealt with the building of the first moon rocket, another with the Russian conquest of America (a popular item in the Joe McCarthy period), a third with the take-over of America by Mafia-type gangsters.

The third might seem to be timely until you consider that the Mafia at its alleged strongest is mighty small potatoes compared with the military-industrial complex about which the late President Eisenhower warned in his farewell address.

No, it is in his short stories that the pure poison exists. *Shark Ship*, an appalling story about the future, is indeed his blackest —and possibly one of the last stories he was to write. Anyone reading that tale and believing that this could be a true depiction of the future would be justified in declining to continue living. Could there be a society so vicious, so without "redeeming merit" as this? In the blackest period of human history—and there have been many—I do not think a philosophy as pervasively inhuman as this could exist.

There are others. There is *Two Dooms*, in which Kornbluth justifies the creation and use of the atomic bomb as the better alternative to what he described as the victory of the enemies in World War II. A hint here of his nonrecovery from the psychosis of military combat—it was written in 1958, a long time after that madness.

I remember especially *The Marching Morons*, based on the idea that, since low-intelligence people breed more children than better educated couples, the world will someday find a tiny hard-worked elite of normal 100 and 100 plus IQ people slaving away to keep a 99 percent majority of subnormals from starving to death. Kornbluth had one bit in there which struck me with more than usual impact: he described a car which was superstreamlined with a fake speedometer showing speeds of 200 miles an hour, while the car was only capable of really running a safe 25! Adding to the illusion for the moronic drivers of these cars was a device which created a dramatic *vroom* noise as if a gale were rushing past the car. This "got" to me when a recently purchased electric coffeepot turned out to have a noisemaker concealed in its base which made a boiling sound as soon as you plugged it in and obviously long before it really could have come to a perk!

Of course, considering the premises I have already stressed in this book, it is possible that the engineer who designed that percolator was a science-fiction reader and had got the idea from Kornbluth. The more I think of it, the more I think it probable.

The thing about Kornbluth's bitterest works is that he seems to have been ahead of the game by a dozen or more years. Some of the despair that shows up today in writers who contemplate the rest of this century was visible in Kornbluth way back then, long before anyone else. Whatever was the cause, it produced a mind and soul so embittered with the world around it and with its inhabitants that it is actually hard for me to conceive how he could have lasted much longer in it.

I recall having the reaction, after reading his final book of short stories, that this mind and the Earth simply could not coexist. One had to go. And since it is Nature that is infinitely the stronger, it was Kornbluth who had to exit. Which he did, dying suddenly of a heart attack at the age of thirty-five in 1958.

This sounds mystical, I know. Is it possible to become so alienated that life itself can no longer be an acceptable alternative? Viewing the subworld of drug addicts and LSD escapists and nut cultists, the drifting alienated psychotics of the so-called underground youth, I believe it possible. There is still among the majority of these that element of faith and hope—the flower children, the rebels, the commune organizers, and the poets still flourish, but the dark traces of the mind blowers streak the scene with the same sort of alienation.

On the other hand, a skepticism as to the merit of science and its future need not produce a sour viewpoint, as witness the satirical writings of Robert Sheckley.

19

The Darkest of Nights

ROBERT SHECKLEY a downbeat writer? Author of anti-Utopias? Yes, because one of the most effective ways of killing a thing is to laugh it to death, and this Sheckley does with vim and originality. His work is light, you could say frothy, and his view is, in its own way, as diabolically "anti" as anything Kornbluth would have dreamed up. But, whereas Kornbluth was sadistically agin' the future, Sheckley is amusingly agin' it. To him it is a potpourri of the same things most odious on Earth, drawn out in such a way as to seem less than real and laughable. The joke is always on us. This is what we value—see how silly it is on a cosmic scale.

Consider his novel *Dimension of Miracles.* Here is an average present-day man who awakens one night to learn he has been the winner of some sort of cosmic lottery—and is taken forthwith to some central depot in what is clearly a present-time existing galactic federative setup, and given his award. He has a hard time figuring out what is going on as naturally he's rather backward compared with all those advanced types, human and inhuman, but his award tries to help. It is a Prize, a living thing with a sarcastic tongue, a presumably wide knowledge, and a diabolical philosophy. As the poor man tries to get home with his Prize he finds that no one has made provision for that safe return. So away he goes in and out of an Alice in Wonderland cosmic madhouse, getting the facts of life in a thoroughly sardonic fashion. He meets a God, acquires a Nemesis, spends time in a perfect Utopian city (which proves to be quite a nightmare), and ends up in a museum of human waste whose motto is "Wastefulness in the defense of luxury is no vice; moderation in the dissemination of excess is no virtue."

We are told (I cannot resist quoting here) that the museum

"was designed by the architect Delvanuey, who also planned Death Trap 66, the famous New York toll road which no one has succeeded in driving from start to finish without accident. This same Delvanuey, you may recall, drew up the plans for Flash Point Towers, Chicago's newest slum, the only slum in the world in which form follows function; that is to say, the first slum which is proudly and avowedly designed *as* a slum."

On the little matter of overpopulation his novelette *The People Trap* says it all in much the same way as Brunner and Harrison do and manages to make it a mad farce. It all takes place on Land Race Day somewhere in the next century when the grand award of an actual acre of land and a house of one's own is given to the first ten men to reach Times Square from Hoboken, New Jersey, after they have passed an exhaustive elimination contest just to be entered in the race. The trip of our hero to his goal, a matter of 5.7 miles, takes him many many days and is a journey which makes Stanley's travels in Darkest Africa seem like a Sunday picnic. Going through the people-packed, jungle-savage streets of Darkest Manhattan is an experience that anyone else would have played as the most frightening of nightmares. But Sheckley does not permit the nightmare to be seen, save obliquely. He touches the surface aspects, he introduces with a light hand the sort of murder that would make a modern gang leader flinch, and he makes it stick. How can you argue with the scene? It is no more than an extension of things plainly in early growth form right now. When our hero wins—where's his acre? On the nearly vertical side of a barren Western desert mountain—that's all that's left of unoccupied land. Asimov spelled it out statistically—that's how it's going to be in only a century if we don't act. Sheckley painted the picture to the statistics.

Funny, yes. Anti-Utopian? To be sure. How else could you read it? Is this what the future is to be like? Is this what the galaxy is to be like? A further development of all our follies and mistakes?

The theme is carried further and more explicitly in a novel which I consider the most completely despairing in the whole of modern science fiction. This is the novel *Out of the Mouth of the Dragon,* the work of a young college graduate named Mark

Geston. It is Geston's second novel; his first was *Lords of the Starship,* the story of a future effort to rebuild civilization which ends in betrayal and world catastrophe.

Out of the Mouth of the Dragon starts a thousand or so years after that one left off. The place is Earth or a planet so similar as to make no difference. The time from our viewpoint must be several thousands of years in the future. The world is a place of ruins and memories and the records of endless failures. The population has diminished due to a series of recurring wars, a series of calls to Armageddon in each of which humanity is exhorted to go to battle in the sacred cause of destroying once and for all the Forces of Evil. Each successive Armageddon turns out to be a fraud, each is a disaster which sets humanity back further and further and saps the remaining strength of a near-licked and finished world.

The story is the account of the last such call to Holy Combat. Once again the last idealists, the last remaining young men who have faith, are roused from their half-empty cities and urged to go once more to the place of combat, to join the army that is to defeat that old enemy (who is never seen and never described). A young man follows such a prophet and once again the armies assemble—and are betrayed. Half-mad, the volunteer wanders over the world accompanied by a ghastly crew and as he wanders he sees that humanity has carried its last straw, it is finished, the world is finished, God is really now dead, and the universe is drying up and cracking up, and it is the absolute end of all hope.

A remarkable work, and especially potent when one considers that this is a novel that came from a member of the youngest generation, for Geston is in his early twenties. Is it possible that this is how an observant and sensitive young man of middle-class background, good education, and culture sees the future of the world he finds himself living in? The answer is obviously that it is.

Samuel R. Delany, at much the same age but with a widely different background, has turned out marvelous novels full of poetry and imagery which also envision a world of half ruins and mutated beings following the disasters of atomic war and cosmic tamperings. But Delany never loses his faith in the survival of art and song and beauty. Geston is capable of appreciating these things but sees no future for them any more than for the rest of the paraphernalia of civilization.

There is an unforgettable scene in *Out of the Mouth of the Dragon* when its half-crazed protagonist returns after seven years of wandering to the devastation of the last battlefield and in a moment of drunken inspiration sets up a banquet table amid the wreckage. About this he gathers twelve skeletons from the slaughter, dresses them in shreds of their old uniforms, props them up, and with himself as the thirteenth, makes a hideous parody of the Last Supper. Here, after nights of madness, the prosthetic voice box of one of the dead speaks to him of first causes and last responses:

> "And do you know what all this progressively more wretched Creation means? . . . It means that the thing which had given life to all of this in the first place and which had conceived of all the plans is a poor, stupid, fumbling idiot just like the rest of us!
>
> "Ah, that *is* beautiful! Think of it! The final basis for a million years of theology and a thousand years of philosophy—nothing more than a useless pile of shit! Noble minds striding the earth, putting their ascetic necks on the block in the name of something which didn't exist. Wars, evolutions, inquisitions, pain, pain: because it was part of the plan, the divinely inspired plan—so full of eternal wisdom that it sickens me now—and therefore how could it be bad?"

This is about as plain a statement of the most nihilistic view of the modern youngest generation as can be found. How representative is it?

I can recognize it in many facets of the so-called underground. It is there like a dark streak discoloring much that these flower children seem to be fighting for. But it is not the dominant view. There is still an overwhelming spirit that believes in a better future—and I will turn away from these spokesmen of negation and get on to the majority writers of science fiction.

20

Toward Galactic Maturity

AS THE CRISIS of the decade of the seventies continues—and continues to darken as surely it must—I have no doubt that the volume and percentage of pessimistic science fiction will increase. But I do not believe that it will ever overcome the immense lead that what I would call optimistic science fiction has. In fact, I am of the opinion that because of the very escapist nature of the science-fiction reader it could not. Too vast a volume of gloom would simply turn these sensitive readers away.

By optimistic science fiction I mean that which regards the future not with horror but as a place for the continuing exploits of humanity, singly or en masse, following the pattern I outlined in the eight phases of the future as unfolded through the medium of a thousand science-fiction fantasists.

Cyril Kornbluth, directly after returning from the war, spent three years with the Chicago bureau of a national press service. Anyone who knows that news-gathering field will realize that too close an acquaintance with the daily petty mishaps, villainies, and miseries of ordinary life could depress anyone—and the news medium is the place to become familiar with much more of it than anyone would reasonably wish to know. This familiarity may have been a factor in Kornbluth's implied resignation from the human race. Then consider the much greater news background of Clifford D. Simak.

Simak has been a journalist all his life and was for many years the news editor of a large metropolitan daily, during the course of which he must have been doused in all the daily human disasters possible. Yet for all that his writings reflect a positive and utterly compassionate sense of the joy of life, of man with nature, and of the infinity of the universe.

While his stories cover the entire scope of the field—from the immediate present to the days of galactic humanity—they seem always to reflect a fine touch for the essential humanness of things, for the small pleasures of daily living, for love and unity with nature. To be sure, Simak's audience, that audience of which we have been speaking all along, has responded with appreciation. Two of his books have won the highest awards of organized s-f fandom, *City* and *Way Station*, two books which incidentally are also among my own favorites.

City (an abominably misleading title, by the way) is a collection of eight episodes in the history of a family, ranging from the near future to ten thousand years from now. It is told as gathered together by man's inheritors and descendants on Earth, those whom we regard as our best friends today, namely, Dogs. The dogs, bred for intelligence, gradually take over our cities, our homes, as we human beings begin to spread into the universe, and *City* becomes in effect a sort of Doggy Bible—here is the legendry of our ancestry, and our makers scattered to the stars to take up life beyond our comprehension. A perfect presentation of the galactic infinite future but handled from a unique point of view.

Humanity develops and builds its robots and trains its canine friends. So the tale unfolds as robot servants, ever faithful, and dogs, ever reverent, remain behind to take the Earth for themselves. As for humanity, we have gone a-roving—to Jupiter, to the stars, changing forms for different planets, outward bound forever.

Here no atomic threat will blast our planet. Here the questions of overpopulation will solve themselves—to be honest, the book was mainly written before these things became manifest problems—but the book still sells well and is still a moving experience.

Way Station, written more than a dozen years later, is Simak's philosophical analysis of the situation of the world today and of the galactic future. A simpler story by far than *City*, it could almost have been compressed into a novelette save for the care and concern Simak takes in developing his personalities and calmly reviewing the situation.

There is, we learn, an already existing Inter-Galactic Council, a union of civilized planets numbering thousands. The Earth, in its twentieth-century stage, is not ready for such acceptance—our part of this galaxy is on an outlying and sparsely starred arm of the Milky Way (which is true). But the needs of interstellar commerce require that a way station be planted on Earth for the transshipment of travelers and products from one planet to another in our sector. This is not done by space flight but by some form of dimensional or supra-Einsteinian technique far beyond our present scientific abilities. As at a relay station, things are received at this building on Earth, rested up, then rephased and sent off again.

A man is required to maintain this station—which exists unknown to human civilization. *Way Station* is the story of this man, the manager of the Earth relay post, of his solitary life, of his daily work, of the love in his life, of the crisis that comes to him when eventually the government's secret agencies begin to pry into the mysterious goings-on in his isolated Wisconsin station.

Simak uses this as a platform to discuss the meaning of interstellar civilization, of the universality of life and hence the universality of tolerance, and of the particular provincial backwardnesses that mark our present existence. The same problems that defeated a Kornbluth, brought a Geston to despair, and reduced a Sheckley to sarcastic laughter are shown to be simply factors that every intelligent race, growing to maturity, must consider, work out, and reduce to a proper historical perspective.

In the historical perspective of millions of years of evolution upward and millions of years of cosmic maturity, perhaps we are now going through no more than a series of minor tests. We have overcome before—thousands of times before—and we have the capacity to overcome now.

Which is not to say that the galactic civilizations are all idealistic Utopias. Far from it; the travelers passing through Earth's secret relay office tell of many crises, of political arguments, hint at trouble. No, Utopia is not in sight but there is the unending conflict of intelligence against nature, which alone is eternal and which alone is worth the game of life.

Such is Clifford Simak, as I read him, and this feel for the galactic and for the strictly human is a combination hard to match.

All of his novels and short stories are eminently readable, all are varied, some are facetious, some minor, and some strike moods and notes similar to the two I prize above the others.

21

Sailors of the Cosmic Seas

CONSIDER another writer of great consistency who has not won any awards, who is a lesser star in the heavens, but whose works in their own way remain true to the galactic future and to a belief in humanity. I refer to A. Bertram Chandler.

Chandler has been turning out good space opera for perhaps thirty years. He himself is a merchant seaman; we understand that these days he has achieved the status of ship's captain and commands a freight liner on the lonely route between Australia and New Zealand. This gives him two advantages over most writers of space-action adventure—he has the long hours of quiet and solitude necessary to dream out his tales of space captains and space explorers on the worlds of the galactic Rim off there in the future times of the Galactic Empire, and it also gives him the extra touch of authenticity that connects the sailors of the seas with those coming sailors of the cosmic oceans.

His space liners are sea liners transposed and transformed. His principal hero, one Grimes, rising from ensign to commander in the Rim Worlds Confederacy, must resemble his creator in more ways than one. No one could write so steadily of a single hero and not reflect himself in him—as indeed Chandler has the audacity to admit in one sequence wherein Grimes has a recession in time and meets up with his own writer!

Chandler's is the world of the Galactic Empire in full flow. Not one empire exactly—there are, we learn, several smaller autarchies, including the lone worlds at the very edge of the Milky Way, facing the vast gap of the cosmos whose other shores are the unattainable galaxies beyond. Here go the space liners, the naval ships of the Empire, the lone cutters of the small independent worlds, the far-faring freighters that journey from world to outlying world on trade. Here are people, colonized from old Earth, and beings born out there who partake of many alien things.

Here, too, is what must have often moved Chandler on his lonely routes across Earth's vastest ocean, where on the south lies the mysterious and mostly unexplored coast of the Last Continent, Antarctica, and on his north, the endless stretches of sea dotted here and there with tiny isles of wonder and mystery. And so we travel with Grimes as on one side lies the awful emptiness of intergalactic space and on the other lie the lost planets of far and isolated stars.

Chandler has worked out a fascinating gimmick to beat the speed-of-light limitation. His ships are equipped with a drive that moves the vessels back in time as they go forward in space. By thus moving along another dimension they make trips which might take many years into voyages of a few days or weeks. This gimmick also allows Chandler to delve into near-Fortean wonders of dimension and alternate worlds—for any such playing with the enigma of time-motion upsets the equilibrium of the universe we were born in—and accidents of the time drive account for many of Chandler's best space adventures.

Other writers have dealt with galactic travel and with colonized worlds, but none so consistently and thoroughly with one special range and segment of the imperial future. Yet of Chandler's dozens of novels and innumerable tales there is none I can single out above the others, and therefore none that has ever forced itself upon fandom as candidates for awards or for listing among the favorites. All his works are of a whole, yet all are individuals of equal interest. One reads Chandler to enjoy, not to cherish, and yet one cannot but get that sense of the infinite secrets of the sea as transposed to the celestial oceans of the sky.

The same is in a manner of speaking true of the work of Cordwainer Smith, the pen name used by the late Paul Linebarger for his books of the future. One cannot name any single Cordwainer Smith book as more outstanding and memorable than any other, and yet all are on a par. The secret is the same as

Chandler's—they are all part of a whole, but unlike Chandler's space opera the Cordwainer tales are not limited to the one factor of space travel. Rather they are a constantly shifting kaleidoscope of wonders in a galactic civilization that is truly of the future—it is no more a reflection of today than today would be a reflection of the Roman Empire. Everything is definitely of that future and part of it, advanced beyond ours by the evolution of time and society.

When I first started reading stories by Cordwainer Smith I wondered at the many loose-ended items he would slip into a story—odd references which seemed to be merely whimsical background bits. But as the stories continued to appear, as books were constructed from the various magazine parts, it became clear that nothing was without its significance. As with a gigantic jigsaw puzzle, every apparently meaningless segment belonged somewhere and referred to something.

I would dearly like to see the entire work of Cordwainer Smith gathered together in one single huge volume, put together in sequence. It would then develop as a unity. For what this amazingly talented man wrote was just that—one huge novel, potentially larger than the *Lord of the Rings* and even more complex. I fear, however, that what might have been the climax of the book was never written and what might then take shape might be a book leading up to something but never reaching it. Such is the danger of writing one connected cosmology when one's life span turns out to be shorter than one estimated.

When does this vast story take place? Sometime perhaps twenty thousand years from now—during the period of the Galactic Empire. Mankind has spread out onto dozens of worlds and the whole is held together by some sort of elite (hereditary? financial? this is not clear) known as The Instrumentality. Mankind has spread out in other ways too. Rather than robots, our ranks have been implemented by the surgical creation of *underpeople,* beasts transformed into human shapes and humanoid minds, yet kept on the servant level, counselors sometimes, slaves most of the time. Some of these underpeople, such as the marvelous cat-woman C'mell, are far from being "under."

And the worlds themselves—each different, each a jewel of

some fabulous sort, each logical in a weird intricate way. Old North Australia, a planet with a monopoly on a crop worth billions, a simple farming world, whose every citizen is wealthier than anyone could dream elsewhere, one of whose citizens wins enough money on the market in one night to go back to old Earth and simply *buy* it! But buying Earth turns out to be no simple transaction—the place is a Pandora's box of complexities and enigmas. *The Planet Buyer* and its sequel *The Underpeople* tell that story—they should be one book; instead they are two relatively undistinguished paperbacks.

Quest of the Three Worlds is another evidence of Cordwainer Smith's patterning. I published this book and I recall that when I had first read the four novelettes that combined to make it I had not realized they were all one novel. Yet they are. Each novel so attained only poses the problems of further works for none are without their unexplained minor mysteries—and with Cordwainer Smith, each is the seed of a new wonder growth.

The man who wrote under the name of Cordwainer Smith was a hardheaded diplomat, no left-winger, an adviser to the State Department, a supporter of Chiang Kai-shek. But despite this, there is nothing at all Vernian about his work. This is socially conscious, wonderfully alive writing. It achieves all this without being in any way of the Left. Such is the special talent of science fiction—that it alone can produce writers with vivid sparkling imaginations, a clearly visible love of the world and of its people, who have managed to be impervious to the lures of Utopian socialism.

Is this a good thing? I don't know. I cannot think of any other field of literature of which this could be said. In this day and age, when so much of the Left is bogged down in disillusion and so much of the Right smells of warmongering and defense hysteria, it is a rather remarkable thing that even those who firmly believe in the System as it is, in capitalism as it is supposed to be (free, opportunity-open, pioneering), can produce singing dreams of infinite mankind and the open cosmos.

22

"*We'll make a star or die trying!*"

CONSIDER one of the finest storytellers in the field, Poul Anderson. In the councils of the science-fiction writers he is of the Right. In the pages of his stories he sings of many futures, varied, near and far, galactic, and beyond the Galactic Empire, of exploration unending, of courage and of derring-do. One of his favorite heroes is a hardheaded entrepreneur of the old piratical variety, the Dutchman Nicholas van Rijn, who, living in the days of the early Galactic Empire, maneuvers his financial affairs with cunning and boldness on planets old and new. Here is an Astor or a Vanderbilt transformed into the far future—believable because such men have existed and do exist, and if the future is capitalist they will exist.

Another of his heroes is Dominic Flandry, a diplomat of the declining days of the Galactic Empire, of the times when corruption and decadence mark the coming end. Flandry himself, not unmarked by decadence, uses his wits and the weakening science of a corrupt empire to stave off the end, to confront inhuman aliens, and to keep the flag of humanity flying.

And after the Empire? Poul Anderson is intrigued by the ancient Vikings, being of Scandinavian ancestry, and in such a novel as *Star Ways* treats of raiders of space, nomad space ships living a free gypsy-Viking sort of life. In other works he deals with the new barbarians that may arise as the edges of civilized space crumble. We have a great variety in Poul Anderson, and he is a writer with color and skill, a tale-teller worthy of his saga-singing ancestry.

Arthur C. Clarke, who as far as I can tell is visibly neither of the Left nor of the Right, has become the best publicized science-fiction writer in the world. He has become the name one is most likely to hear when mainstream sources, unfamiliar with the field, choose an example of an s-f writer. Clarke is known today as the man who wrote *2001,* the movie that cost more and satisfied less than any other fantasy film yet produced. But to me Clarke means far more than this.

He is, for instance, credited with doing more than any other single writer to popularize and publicize space flight. He was active in the organization of rocket experimenter societies back in the days when it was unfashionable and in the public eye improbable. Some of his early novels dealt with that, novels I must confess I found not too interesting. For me Clarke was at his very best when he let his imagination wander far from the fields of real technology. One of his earliest books, a brilliant fantasy of the very far future, *Against the Fall of Night,* is virtually a prose poem of the last days of Earth and faith in man's immortality. A billion years from now, after man's empire has encompassed the universe, time has eroded it again, and there is but the one last city left where the last men dream and go their haunted way.

But the universe does not end here. For in this last city the last act is to send a message out into the universe where somewhere there must still be men to carry the word that Mankind would come back. A beautiful book, an act of faith for a science-fiction mind.

Childhood's End is Clarke's most famous novel. This tale of the new evolution of a generation of human children into something higher, managed and manipulated by peacemakers from outer space, has always seemed to me to be a novel of despair. Others may see it as offering hope, but this tampering with humanity always struck me as being synthetic, as being not of a par with Stapledon's new men, not to mention others who have attempted the theme.

Like most of the older generation of science-fiction writers and fans, I knew Clarke back when we were all just struggling fans, a tiny minority of beleaguered space voyagers. Fame and fortune came to him because of the technical faith he had in interplanetary flight first and because of the variety of his concepts in short tales of the immediate space adventures to come. Though he wrote of the period I have described as the Challenge to God, his fame came from the very first period, that of the first flights.

At this point it is imperative to mention Ray Bradbury, whose paperback editions now bear the quotation: "The world's greatest living science fiction writer." I can find no mention of the author of this quote, but no matter—it could be any of hundreds of reviewers from the mainstream press, taken by the skill and beauty of Bradbury's work, carried away by his intensely poetic fantasy and emotional impact, and entirely unaware that Ray Bradbury is not really a science-fiction writer at all.

Only a very small percentage of Bradbury's works can be classified as science fiction. Although his most "science-fictional" book, *The Martian Chronicles,* is a classic, its s-f plausibility is slight. Essentially (like almost all his books) a compilation of short stories (many of which originally appeared in s-f magazines) and roughly making a panorama of the next century, it has the form of science fiction but in content there is no effort to implement the factual backgrounds. His Mars bears no relation to the astronomical planet. His stories are stories of people —real and honest and true in their understanding of human nature—but for his purposes the trappings of science fiction are sufficient—mere stage settings.

Ray Bradbury is essentially a doomsman where the future is concerned. He distrusts science, distrusts technology, fears the complexity of a world deriving its substance from these things. He longs for the presumed simplicity of a past century and the innocence of boyhood. None of his work has impinged on the galactic cosmology of an Asimov or a Stapledon. He is outside the field—a mainstream fantasist of great brilliance, a literary warrior in an allied way against the three dooms of our century, an associate of the Wellsian concept, but certainly not "the world's greatest living science fiction writer."

If anyone could be said to have a claim to that sort of title, it could possibly be Robert A. Heinlein.

Like Poul Anderson, he is generally credited with being of the political Right, and he is also a storyteller of such talent that his novels outsell all others and his name remains fixed at the top of every list of favorites. Whether he is truly of the political

Right I am not so ready to say. It is an easy shibboleth, but dangerous. Heinlein himself has warned people not to judge his personal opinions by the attitudes and dialogues of the characters in his various stories. He may be right.

Farnham's Freehold may appear to be a firm bit of flag-waving fixed patriotism, but how can you square it with *Stranger in a Strange Land?* When the hippies and rebel youngsters of Haight-Ashbury and the other free communities of youth take the latter work as one of their Bibles, organize water-brotherhood societies, and pick up *grok* as a favored word, where can you say the author stands? When the latter work seems to present a case for free love, for free emotions, for standing aloof from the stiff formalized "civilization" of the stuffy older generations, can you call its author a rightist?

Maybe he is. I will not say that there isn't a case to be made for it. He is an Annapolis graduate, certainly a believer in free enterprise, and the bulk of his writings seem to reflect a viewpoint not too dissimilar to the economic-patriotic views of *Analog* magazine. But I can take it from Heinlein whereas I cannot take it from John Campbell. I know that Robert Heinlein did study the economic systems of the world, did investigate and see for himself the workings of many systems and the minds of advocates of all types of systems. In Bob Heinlein we have an extraordinarily sharp-eyed observer of the human world.

I would not advise being too quick to pin any label on Heinlein. I suspect that his views are always his own—that they parallel various viewpoints, usually right wing, but that they are not *of* the Right. Heinlein is first and foremost a free mind. It is as such that I read him. I do not necessarily like all that I read and I do not agree with a number of the viewpoints his characters express.

I found *Starship Troopers* militaristic and personally distasteful—but a good case can be made for the special rights of men who lay their lives on the line for their country, their people, their planet. When a book such as that also wins the Hugo for the best s-f novel of the year by the vote of readers and writers it would appear that Heinlein made his argument (as per that book) with the skill and wonder-creating ability which is his trademark.

To take an unpleasant proposition and make people like it, that is talent. Perhaps it might also be something that would make propagandists of the Left say such a man is to be feared and fought.

But then account for the whacky nihilism and hero-wrecking of *Glory Road* and the hippie-acceptance of *Stranger in a Strange Land*. Account for the faith in space of *The Man Who Sold the Moon* and for the exposure of religious fanaticism implicit in *Revolt in 2100* (a book which could be dynamite if Scientology or Jehovah's Witnesses ever had their way).

As far as I am concerned, Robert A. Heinlein is a universe maker who believes in the future of mankind and in the endless frontier of the galactic civilization that is to be. In this day of despair and crises, that faith is more of a true beacon than all the frightened philosophies of the panicked dystopians.

Look through the bulk of his novels and you will find that faith always shining through. Whatever the nature of the novel, whatever his message may be, this is the one constant that Heinlein will not surrender. Humanity, whatever its faults, is the best darned thing going and will never be pinned to the mat.

I riffle through his many juvenile novels—a collection that has influenced who knows how many minds that are now mature and working—and I recall a passage in one of the best, entitled *Have Space Suit—Will Travel*. A teen-ager acquires a space suit and then by a series of mischances and bold adventures goes out into the universe among aliens, eventually to find himself placed on trial, as spokesman for mankind before the Council of the Three Galaxies—a police body, not a government, whose concern is that humanity is a dangerous warmaking destructive race that ought to be exterminated before it becomes a menace to other intelligences on other worlds.

The outlook seems hopeless, for out of the boy's own mouth have been taped honest discussions of the black marks of our human past—wars and crusades and concentration camps. Desperate, the boy, considering the whole thing unfair, for he never sought to be the world's sole attorney at a trial, where all, the world itself, is in the balance, does his best. But at last, sensing that the trial is going against Earth:

> I looked around at the hall. . . . "Just this!" I said savagely. "It's not a defense, you don't *want* a defense. All right, take away our star—you will if you can and I guess you can. Go ahead! We'll *make* a star! Then, someday, we'll come back and hunt you down —all of you!"
>
> Nobody bawled me out. I suddenly felt like a kid who has made a horrible mistake at a party and doesn't know how to cover it up. But I meant it. Oh, I didn't think we could *do* it. Not yet. But we'd *try*. "Die trying" is the proudest human thing.

"We'll make a star or die trying," says Heinlein—and in their own way so say Simak and Chandler and Smith and Anderson and a myriad others who fill the pages of the real science-fiction magazines and the real science-fiction books that crowd the newsstands and bookstores of the world.

23

Après Nous le Déluge

DIAMETRICALLY OPPOSITE to this determined galactic optimism is the message that underlies the movement in science fiction known as the New Wave. Originating several years ago in London, and still mainly centered, as far as conscious editorial direction is concerned, around the British magazine *New Worlds*, it has aroused a great deal of controversy and discussion among science-fiction writers and readers.

New Worlds was originally a standard old-line science-fiction monthly that had appeared for many years edited by the distinguished science-fiction authority Edward John Carnell. But when Carnell stepped down as editor of the magazine, Michael Moorcock took the post and began to alter the policy of the magazine, as well as to redesign its entire appearance externally and internally.

Moorcock, himself a capable and talented writer, turned out to have some very different ideas about the future of science fiction, and these ideas rapidly made themselves known as the New Wave began to take shape and even to assume some of the aspects of a crusade.

Primarily we had once again the effort to merge science fiction into the mainstream of literature. This time the attempt was made in a much more organized and effective form. The charges brought against old-line science fiction were on the basis of both structure and content. Structurally the charge was made that too much of the writing retained the flavor of the pulps, that science-fiction writers were not keeping up with the experimental avant-garde of the literary world—the William Burroughs and Allen Ginsberg schools, for instance.

Internally the charge was made that science fiction actually was dead—because the future was no longer credible. The crises of the twentieth century—the Bomb, overpopulation, pollution— were obviously insurmountable. We would all never make it into the twenty-first century. This being so, these dreams of inter-planetary colonies, of technological things to come, of galactic empires, and so on were reduced to the status of pure fantasy— they could not be considered scientifically credible since they had been canceled out by the coming end of civilization and the world.

Hence science fiction as it had been during the forties and fifties had been swept aside by the facts of history of the sixties and seventies. *New Worlds* started to refer to "S-F" as meaning Speculative Fiction, a term they conceived to have more leeway and less "science."

Thus *New Worlds* and the writers associated with it began a campaign to change the nature of s-f. If you could not seriously believe in the future, all systems were no-go. Hence the realm of such literature was in that of the avant-garde—which is to say, let the readers and writers that used to dream of galactic futures now get their kicks out of experimental styles of writing, the free discussion of sex, the overthrow of all standards and morals (since, if the world is going to end, what merit had these things?).

Now, there was something to be said for improving the style of science fiction, of bringing it further away from its pulp origins, of adopting the best elements of the newest literary techniques if and when applicable. The best of the New Wave writers, J. G. Ballard, had never been in the pulp tradition, had always maintained some status with the British literary mainstream. But Ballard had, it must be noted, also always been a writer of doomed-world stories. None of his novels had ever fitted into the galactic tradition outlined in this study. All had been novels of the near future wherein the world faced total disaster of various types. Ballard needed no convincing to accept the full premise of the *New Worlds* message.

Brian Aldiss, a writer of the finest science-fiction talents, was the other major convert. He began a series of Joycean tales in *New Worlds*, which were eventually to collate into his book *Barefoot in the Head*, possibly his least comprehensible s-f work—a novel of hallucinatory passages, double images, Joycean constructions, and so on. After which, Aldiss went directly into the mainstream with a novel, *The Hand-Reared Boy*, which had no fantasy content whatever and made the best sellers on the basis of its sexual connotations.

The best—or perhaps it ought to be the worst—example of the New Wave is embodied in the novels and tales of a compound character called Jerry Cornelius—produced in a mélange of styles, chaotic plotting, and a chameleon of a protagonist who occasionally combines the characteristics of such as James Bond, Dr. Frankenstein, the Chevalier D'Eon, Jack the Ripper, and whatever else comes to mind. *The Final Programme* by Michael Moorcock was the first Jerry Cornelius novel to appear in book form—but other writers have been allowed to use the character in pieces of varying length and wild variety remarkably reminiscent of the sort of thing one finds in high school parodies.

The New Wave did some good—it did help to bring about an awareness of stylistic possibilities and thus to broaden the base of some of the more talented writers, such as Samuel R. Delany, Norman Spinrad, and possibly even John Brunner. But by and large it has begun to fade out due to its own negative outlook.

The *New Worlds* group certainly came from the Wellsian tradition, but they represent a group of socially sensitive writers who have decided that the battle for the future is a lost cause. In the tradition of *après nous le déluge* thinking, the sensual pleasures come to the fore as the only immediate real values left. Hence a great deal of the New Wave writing concerns itself with shock words and shock scenes, hallucinatory fantasies, and sex.

The New Wave represents a departure from the science-fiction directives for mankind, and its most devoted advocates have ceased to be universe makers.

24

Defy the Devil

BUT DO WE have any universe makers who seem to be of the New Wave? Some point to Harlan Ellison. In fact, on one of his books, *The New Yorker* is quoted as calling him "the chief prophet of the New Wave."

I think they are wrong, and as far as I know Harlan Ellison does not identify himself with the New Wave. He would be writing his kind of stories just the way he is writing them if there had never been a *New Worlds* magazine, or a Michael Moorcock or a Judith Merril, whose annual anthologies were the first heralds of the coming of the cult.

Harlan Ellison is one of those one-man phenomena who pop up in a field, follow their own rules, and have such a terrific charisma and personal drive that they get away with it. They break all the rules and make the rest like it. He is in an Asimovian sense a "mule," a unique sort of genius who can lead where others can never successfully follow, who can hold an audience enthralled yet never gain a convert, who can insult and have only the stupid offended.

New Wave—in the sense that Harlan Ellison's short stories have most certainly charted new paths in writing, in that he has indeed found new ultramodern ways of narration which yet manage to keep comprehension (compared with most of the New Wave pioneering which actually reverts back to antiquated experimental styles of the twenties and thirties without acknowledging it; a great deal of the New Wave material smacks of Dadaism, a 1919–1920 manifestation), in that he takes the downbeat view of the far future and therefore, by implication, seems to accept the view that there is no real hope for humanity and that we are not going to surmount the crises of this century.

In that sense Harlan Ellison is New Wave, and if so, is the best of them all.

Harlan, who started being noticed when he was but a kid fan, never stopped running. A bundle of incredible vitality, he has had more than twenty books published—collections of his over six hundred short stories—has carried off awards in whatever fields he has chosen to conquer, and is still turning out talented material at a great rate. I note that the novel is obviously not his form—he has but one s-f novel on his list of published works.

But the thing that concerns this discussion is Harlan Ellison as a prophet of doom. Ellison has never gone around saying that science fiction is dead and turning up his nose at s-f readers and fans—the implied viewpoint of the New Wavers. He has never proclaimed that his style of writing is the only modern one and everyone else should conform or go back to kindergarten. And he has never stopped defying the future to do its damnedest.

A Wellsian in the sense that I have defined it, he is always concerned with people and society, and anyone who could claim that he had hauled down his flag and was running into some somatic dugout would have to be totally unfamiliar with his work. Yet the fact remains that he is downbeat, that the great majority of his tales are downbeat, that they deal primarily with the next few decades, which are in no way pleasing to contemplate and which, as he depicts them, are quite gosh-darned nightmarish. But since Harlan Ellison is nothing if not exceedingly vocal, let me quote from a couple of places:

"The world you were born into is going nuts. Just check around if you think I'm wrong. . . ."

". . . not Christ nor man nor governments of men will save you . . . writers about tomorrow must stop living in yesterday and work from their hearts and their guts and their courage to tell us about tomorrow, before all the tomorrows are stolen away from us . . . no one will come down from the mountain to save your lily-white hide or your black ass. God is within you. Save yourselves."

(The first is from the flyleaf of his first hard-cover book *Love Ain't Nothing but Sex Misspelled*. The second paragraph is from a paperback anthology, *The Beast That Shouted Love at the Heart of the World*.)

With the essence of that second statement I cannot disagree. It is what I have been saying here. It also defines the difference between Ellison and the Moorcock group—the latter clearly do not believe there will be a tomorrow to save or one that would be worth saving. And Ellison, who, from his stories, probably knows more and understands more about the hideous sides of the present and near future than they ever have, still thinks that there may be something over those stormy hills worth looking for.

25

Why Frodo Lives

STILL I QUESTION whether the constant depiction and reiteration of horrors, both mental and of the immediate future, are exactly the way to rally a fight for the cause of humanity. Considering the audience that science fiction reaches, the primary audience, that is, we have a readership of youth. It is youth in this day and age, we are told by newspapers and pedants, that is being alienated.

On the other hand, would a sort of Pollyanna Utopianism be of any greater merit? Equally unlikely—and the pure sort of idyllic Utopian tale is conspicuous by its absence in the strictly science-fiction output today.

But . . .

But there is something suspiciously like it around and thriving. And that is an allied field of fantasy which is being read by a large section of the science-fiction audience and an equally large section of youth who wouldn't be seen with a copy of *Analog*. I refer to what is called the literature of heroic fantasy, of which a dozen varieties are popping up in paperback books and which is elbowing its way onto the science-fiction racks on newsstands and into the columns of the magazines.

Most of it is scarcely worth looking at. Pulpy, quickly invented imitations of Edgar Rice Burroughs, Robert E. Howard, and J. R. R. Tolkien. Where did it come from? Why—from the popularity of the latter.

I spoke of *The Lord of the Rings* back at the start of this book, just to point out why that magnificent series of novels about Middle Earth cannot qualify for the designation science fiction. It is fantasy, wonderfully contrived, a world worked out in loving detail, a culture depicted with the depth of near-reality. This, however, does not explain why Tolkien's epic became so popular with youth, especially with college youth, and why it has sold in the millions of copies and is presumably still doing so.

It may not be science fiction but it is read and treasured by science-fiction readers. I myself as a member of the small committee of experts that first granted awards in the field, was instrumental in voting the Tolkien work the International Fantasy Award of its year (the Hugo awards came later and were a more popular-based outgrowth of this committee). As such I was guilty perhaps of being a premature Middle Earth enthusiast. In those days, the first year of its appearance in the United States, the Rings novels were available only in very high-priced hard-bound British imports.

I am also guilty of having lit the spark that started the explosion for Tolkien, in so far as it was the editions I initiated and edited that first put Tolkien on the newsstands in low-priced paperback editions.

Those pioneer paperback editions set off a controversy between publishers and fans that made headlines in newspapers and periodicals all over the country. I must admit that I was startled at the heat engendered. Those who felt that Tolkien had somehow been injured by the publishing competition rallied to his name with the ardor one would only expect from religious fanatics. It was clear that, while I, as an editor, could view Tolkien with a certain dispassion (after all, I had passed through my period of prime enthusiasm some years earlier), his newly found mass audience found in him something greater than mere entertainment reading, something you would almost suspect they were ready to die for.

It was a phenomenon one had to think about. Think about it I did, and observed too.

What did the *Lord of the Rings* signify? Why had it touched off such depths of support in its readers?

Looked at superficially, the *Lord of the Rings* novels might be supposed to be some sort of allegory about the rise of the Nazis and the defensive position in the face of that of Britain and France. But since we know that Tolkien started writing his epics long before Hitler, one could still suppose an allegory influencing its author's mind from World War I and the menace of the East against the comfortable shires and homes of Old England.

Tolkien himself has insistently denied this. At first I was inclined to take his denial as meaning that he himself simply wasn't aware of the allegorical significance. But I think now he is right. For what Tolkien did in his work was to write a modern fantasy in the style of the ancient epics of the founders of European civilization. *The Lord of the Rings* is not an allegory —it is of a style and form with Beowulf, the Nibelungen, the Eddas, the sagas of pre-medieval man.

In Middle Earth we have the ingredients of those works in that in the mind of the primitive saga storytellers such things as pure Good and pure Evil exist and are taken for granted. In those days a less sophisticated humanity could believe that there was in the universe an essence that was good and another essence that was evil. No psychological or economic analysis of one's opponents to shed light on their hidden motivations. No self-doubts, no seeking of the flaw in one's own soul, no anti-heroes or honorable villains, no room for weaklings or questioners.

So it is with Tolkien. Sauron is Evil, through and through, and his armies and minions are equally Evil. His motivation is all bad. His victory would be pure disaster, with no alleviating conversions.

Frodo is Good. His friends and companions are Good. Their motivations are unquestionably pure. Their victory is everyone's victory, because they are all that is Good and Sauron is all that is Bad.

Pure Good. Pure Evil. We had thought that in this twentieth-century world such concepts were taboo. Defunct. Compromise is the order of the day—if you can't lick 'em, join 'em.

But the men of a thousand years ago would never have understood that. They knew there was Good and that it had to be fought for.

So, then, what did it mean when thousands of college students, young people of our day and our age, suddenly started chalking on walls and penning on posters and putting on lapel buttons the slogan: "Frodo Lives."

What could it mean but that Good lives?

Good lives!

What does it mean when a thirst for novels wherein unmistakable heroes fight against unmistakable villains continues to show itself in fantasy writings, continues to force itself side by side with science fiction and compete for the same audience?

It means that there is hope for humanity and hope for youth. For it means that hundreds of thousands—possibly millions—of young intelligent people are not basically cynics and victims of despair. It means that the ancient belief in the rightness of innate Good—that belief which sustained all the armies of prehistory whose battles laid the foundations for all that we call civilization and culture—has not died from the human spirit. Youth recognized it when it came to them in its ancient pure form and rallied to it.

Let the New Wave sneer and snarl and cry that science fiction is dead and its vision of galactic futures dead; let them present their writings of despair filled with shock words and shock concepts; they have been defeated already by the cry *Frodo Lives!*

For, if Frodo lives, we shall not despair. However dark the clouds of the twentieth century, the shadow of Evil was equally dark—and, though it may take peril and pain, humanity shall overcome.

That is how I read the meaning of Tolkien.

26

Cosmotropism

I HAVE A THEORY. I think that space flight is not a whim that happened to arise in the minds of dreamers and became practical when rockets were invented for warfare and a lot of government money needed spending. I think that space flight is a condition of Nature that comes into effect when an intelligent species reaches the saturation point of its planetary habitat combined with a certain level of technological ability.

Since the human species had never previously fulfilled those conditions, we have never had occasion to note this outward-movement tropism before. But I think it is a built-in gene-directed drive for the spreading of the species and its continuation.

Let me give you an example of how this might be. If you have ever observed the growth of spore contamination in a Petri dish, you will be familiar with the experiment. Take a Petri dish—a flat dish of highly nutritive matter kept sterile—and expose it briefly to the air. Close it again, set it aside in a warm place, and watch it. Soon spots of dark green or brown or blue will appear on the surface of the nutriment. These are colonies of microscopic plant life, algae, fungi, mold, that have grown from spores which wafted down upon the surface of the culture during the brief period of its exposure to the atmosphere.

As you know, the air of Earth is contaminated with such spores, by the countless trillions of trillions, floating unseen by our eyes wherever there is air. The Petri dish experiment is a common one in elementary science which demonstrates exactly that point.

Let us watch what happens next. We have our re-covered dish with its several colonies of plant life. These grow as the growing vegetation (microscopic but vegetation just the same) pushes outward devouring the nutriment, turning it into new plant life (and also transforming some of it into waste). The several spots grow. They begin to touch each other's borders. There is a brief period of stasis, then they grow around and into each other. In time the Petri dish is one solid surface of mold life and no untouched part of the nutriment can be seen. The mold flourishes. It grows dense. It grows tall. It then flowers—it begins to form spore balls.

Assume that the lid of the dish is taken off. The spore balls reach maturity—they burst and send out into the atmosphere millions and millions of new spore seeds to float away. After this flowering the mold forest begins to diminish. The nutriment of the dish is being exhausted. Some of the mold begins to dry up, to die away. Spots remain alive for a while, but unless new moisture comes, unless the nutriment is renewed, eventually the colony dies away.

Mold life, lichen, fungi—they are not intelligent species. What they do is all gene-programed, totally involuntary, automatic biochemical responses to given conditions. Of the millions of spores sent out from such colonies, how many will come to rest on surfaces conducive to new colonies? One? Two? Some will. Out of trillions whose numbers wander the airs of Earth from pole to pole and as far up as the limits of the stratosphere enough will come to rest to guarantee that the kinds of life that gave birth to them will be continued forever and forever.

But what of the original colonies—those of the Petri dish that sent these spores forth never to return? They vanish eventually. They can know nothing of their seedlings' success or failure. The reproduction of the mold species is an act of Nature that disregards the individual life of the parent plant.

Consider now the planet Earth. Upon its surface there arises an intelligent species which survives all natural disasters including its own various follies and manages to spread its colonies onto every inhabitable spot on Earth. Every continent, every island which can give adequate nutriment to a family of human beings, does so. The isolated colonies of human beings that existed on the planetary surface as of fifty thousand years ago—and the eons that preceded—made contact with each other in the past tens of thousands of years. They touched borders here and there, they clashed, they combined. Now, in this day and age, the earth is one inhabited surface—countries merge daily in commerce and interdependence, and the idea and necessity of merging all governments into a single supergovernment grows in the minds of men until it would seem that in the next century or so—other conditions set aside—there would be only one all-embracing worldwide government.

Consider also that the nutriment of the earth is rapidly being exhausted and that the numbers of humanity are growing to a danger point.

Now note that in the past half century the idea of space flight, which was a whimsy of past centuries, caught hold, became potent, powerful, and in the past three decades became an increasingly dominant factor in technology and social endeavors. A large section of the public funds of the two major powers of Earth is diverted to the development of means of getting into space—and there is strangely little protest from their populations.

What then? Science fiction, increasingly prominent in the concepts of the public and the projections of scientists, points continuously and insistently on exploring the neighboring planets, and on colonizing them if possible. The idea crops up of crossing the light years between our sun and the others around it in huge space ships, designed to carry a village-sized mass of men and women, designed as tiny man-made planets so that these men and women can propagate, raise children, raise the several generations that must live and die before the hundreds of years that it may take that vast ship to cross the gap between one sun and another at less than the speed of light. Such starships travel until they find a habitable planet, and settle thereon, ending their travel of many generations, discharging their cargo of human beings to establish homes on that distant world, to set up towns, to put a human culture there.

The thinking is present. It is now part of the general scene in science-fiction writing. It seems to have first made its appearance some time early in the 1930's—I recall a short story telling of the landing of such a starship with its hundreds of human colonists. I can't recall the title at the moment—it was not a distinguished tale otherwise, and I suspect that even earlier specimens might be found.

Some great novels have been written about such starships, about life aboard them, about the possible disasters that could confront them. Robert A. Heinlein wrote two great novellas *Universe* and *Common Sense* about such a starship—they are reprinted as one in his book *Orphans of the Sky*. Brian Aldiss' first really great s-f novel was such a book, called *Non-Stop* in its original edition, and simply *Star Ship* in its American edition. A recent Nebula winner, Alexei Panshin's *Rite of Passage,* is a particularly outstanding example. Dozens of other examples are available now in great variety and of varying quality.

The idea is accepted. It is part of the science-fiction roots of modern civilization. It will not be too long before the thought of constructing such vessels begins to slip into the halls of politics, first lightly, seemingly facetiously, then seriously. (Note how easily Vice-President Agnew slipped the idea of a manned expedition to Mars in the 1980's into the public eye with no particular gasps of astonishment or objections.)

We stop now to ask why. Starships will not alleviate the overcrowding of Earth. We cannot emigrate to the stars ourselves—only our children's children's children (who will never have known Earth)—and then only in minuscule numbers. What are a few thousand, or even a few tens of thousands of star migrants, when the Earth's population contains billions? Starships will be expensive—they will take a good chunk of any nation's economy. But they will be made. I have no doubt of that.

Because I think—and I think this argument will be used effectively by political leaders—they are humanity's guarantee of cosmic immortality. Once we have spread out beyond the now limited confines of this one habitable planet we—or human beings carrying our genes and our heritage—will become immortal. Let a thousand starships go out and we will be like the spores of the air—our species will go on forever and our memory, that of Earth, will be revered forever.

Because we are not mindless spores, do not forget. The analogy can go only so far. We are as far from the spores on the spectrum of life as we can get. Unlike those simple life forms, we are the only living species of Earth that can notice the stars, that can speculate upon them, that is conscious of past, present, and future, and that can project upon them. We can and we do direct our own fates. We can change nature—we are not totally dependent upon its bounty and doomed to die when we have used it all up. We know of what our Petri dish consists and we know how to conserve it, how to renew it, how to reconstruct it. True, we are bunglers and muddlers at this stage. But we do know how. Time and the pressure of numbers will force us to utilize our knowledge and our intelligent capacities to preserve ourselves here.

We do have this compulsion to go out. We have a conscious drive for immortality—if not of the individual, certainly of the nations and species. Our record is that of a fighting beast of herdlike nature yet of individuality. Our record, shown in a million ways, is that our individuals will sacrifice themselves for the common good—our young men have gone out in a thousand wars and a million tribal feuds before there were wars, and have given their lives in the belief they were fighting to save the lives and preserve the advantages of their kinsmen at home, of their fellow tribesmen, of their fellow countrymen. The man who sacrifices his life for his fellow men does not know whether he has died in vain. He cannot possibly gain personal advantage from his own death. He follows what must be a natural instinct, a human tropism, that programs him to be prepared to fight to the death for a cause he takes on faith to be necessary to his species' survival.

I think the drive to send out starships as spores of humanity is a tropism which, now that we have spread over all the Earth, is come to the fore in human affairs. I can foresee the day, which may be only in the next century or two, when it will be common practice to send up stargoing capsules, each with a dozen men and women, each directed at a star around which we will have cause to believe there are planets which may be habitable. Not blind, as with spores, but intelligently directed. If we can carry such men and women in suspended animation, so much the better. Robotic controls can do the work, automatic sensors can waken the cargo when the time comes.

Or mile-long self-contained starships, miniature worlds in which generations can live and die, may be the way. Whichever will prove most practical, that will humanity do. For it will be our ticket to immortality. It will be the birth of cosmic humanity, of that Galactic Empire which seems to be surely part of the future once we become truly the masters of space flight.

27

Shapers of the Future

NOW I COME TO THE END of this study of science fiction and its meaning in the world. The books and stories I have mentioned barely scratch the surface of the thousands and thousands of tales that have been amassed over the past half century and which compose the body of the field. These works represent in their way the visions of science-and-humanity-oriented minds of the way the world has gone and the ways in which we might go.

There is a rising tide of gloom and concern in the world today and it is reflected in modern science fiction. Yet it is but a tiny countercurrent to the vast movement of ideas that continue to fascinate and grip the minds of the most imaginative people of our day. It can never be otherwise.

Wherever science goes, in whatever direction a discovery seems to point, these are guidelines to the soaring speculations of the science-fiction writers. They seize upon, they examine, and they leap to conclusions that trained experimenters dare not. Their mirrors of the future shape the future. Such speculations, such visions, are not illusions to pass with the change of light, but affect that future. They make their mark, however faint at first, but a real mark nonetheless in the minds of men and the currents of the world.

When I say that science-fiction writing in the vast majority speaks of an infinite range that is about to open to humanity in the universe I say that that very thought reinforces the probability that this will be so. When I say that science-fiction writers believe we will survive whatever catastrophes nature or man may have in store for us, survive or bypass them, that too increases the chances for such survival.

Some anthropologists like to make the claim that humanity is but a very recent thing on this Earth—a mere newcomer whose tenure is measured in a few tens of thousands of years—which is like a second to the history of life on this planet. I say this is nonsense. We are the living descendants of ancestors whose roots go back to the very dawn of life. For the past eight or ten million years our ancestors have been living by their brain power, which has steadily increased as use and recurrent danger honed their wits. We ourselves, living today, are, each one of us, the descendants of the survivors of every disaster that has ever happened—the survivors, I repeat. We have a capacity for survival—by our wits—that should not ever be underrated.

The troubles that loom ahead may seem difficult to overcome, but science-fiction writers have already imagined various ways in which they could be met, by which they could be surmounted, or by means of which we could survive them. Once a thing can be imagined, it can be done—such is the lesson I draw from science fiction.

If we can conceive of it, then it is possible.

If it is possible, then eventually even the dullest among us will see the way when dire necessity compels.

The leaders of nations, the political rulers of the world, are a breed that often seems to be lacking in vivid imagination and not given to fantastic speculation. No matter. These politicians, whatever their philosophy or creed or allegiance, have one thing in common. They are not suicidal. When an issue comes up which threatens their power, their property, their glory, and their lives, they do act. Given the impetus of minds that have seen various ways forward, these leaders have a way of utilizing those programs.

This is the way it is and this is the way it is going to work out.

We live in a world shaped by science fiction and whose future has been charted by science fiction. I have spelled out something of that charting. The outlook is terrific. Whatever may be the personal fate of any specific individual in the years ahead, I have no doubt at all of the fate of the people of the Earth. Everything that has gone before is truly but prehistory.

Whatever may be, I am sure of one thing. There is a famous poem which has the constant refrain, "This is the way the world ends." Well . . .

We are not going to end with a bang.

We are not going to end with a whimper.

We are not going to end.

That's all.

INDEX

71 72 73 74 10 9 8 7 6 5 4 3 2 1